UP FROM
ASHES

UP FROM ASHES
THE STREETS, PRISON, AND REDEMPTION

LARDELL L. SPRATT

Detroit, Michigan
Printed in the United States of America

©2023 Lardell L. Spratt

Publishing services by Tucker Publishing House, LLC

11000 W. McNichols Rd

Suite 323

Detroit, Michigan 48221

www.tuckerpublishinghouse.com

Paperback ISBN 979-8-218-19484-0

No parts of this book may be reproduced without the written consent of the author, Lardell Spratt also known as "LaDell 'Coach Dell' Spratt".

TABLE OF CONTENTS

Introduction vii
Chapter 1 1
Chapter 2 14
Chapter 3 24
Chapter 4 34
Chapter 5 44
Chapter 6 55
Chapter 7 64
Chapter 8 73
Chapter 9 84
Chapter 10 93
Chapter 11 106
Chapter 12 117
Chapter 13 128

Afterword: Up From Ashes 135
Acknowledgments 138
Author Bio 141

CONTENT GUIDANCE

This memoir explores aspects of street life, childhood abuse, and prison violence. Please read with care. In this book, all names mentioned are fictional (except those where permission was granted to use real names) and do not represent any real individuals. Any resemblance to actual people, living or deceased, is purely coincidental.

INTRODUCTION

My world was once ash. Whatever it was that I aspired to be; whatever fleeting dream or ambition to be a positive impact on the world—went up in flames. My environment and upbringing supplied the gasoline, and I lit the flame of my demise. Even still, other opposing forces fanned the flames as my potential continued to burn away. Who was I meant to be? Surely, there was more that I was created to do and become other than another statistic. What purpose did my struggles and even my triumphs serve in the grand scheme of YAH's plan for my life?

I could not see myself beyond what other negative influences decided I should become. Growing up on the west side of Detroit, I didn't witness many positive depictions of Black men. The Heathcliff Huxtables and other Black role models on the TV screen seemed as fictional to me as a talking cat chasing a cunning little mouse. I was born with so many odds stacked against me—poverty, racism, lack of identity, depression, and abuse—that I didn't realize that my world was on fire. The flames eventually warmed me, and the smell of singed objects had become more and more fragrant.

And then the fire consumed me.

I found myself facing an 18-30 year prison sentence simply because I decided to act violently resulting in someone losing their life. It was a cold, impulsive decision, but one that started me on a path of self-discovery and redemption. The United States Criminal Justice system was never designed to truly rehabilitate and reform anyone—yet it was within this system that I was able to face the ugliest, most deeply wounded, and broken parts of myself and decide that I was ready to emerge into something better.

I share my story because I know so many people like me—people who have been living someone else's definition of who they are instead of making that decision for themselves. People who feel like their mistakes have defined them and are unable to see themselves beyond someone else's labels. People who have no hope and feel the call of greatness on their lives, but don't know how to answer that call. My goal is to ignite a spark within you—not the all-consuming one that brings death and destruction—but the kind that gives light and possibilities. Encouraging you to realize that even the most damaged soil can still produce beautiful things.

CHAPTER 1

"Dell...DELL! Get your ass in here right now!"

A chill ripped through my back, and I could feel my blood pumping aggressively through my heart. I didn't know what it could have been this time, but I know that it wasn't going to be good. It must be what a lamb feels like smelling the death of his companions as he awaits his own slaughter.

"DELL!"

I mustered up as much courage as my nine-year-old body could, and I joined her in the living room. I was stiff—bracing myself for the uncertainty and sporadic episodes that my mother would bring about. When I approached her, she had a far-off glaze in her eyes and appeared as though she was in a trance. Inside I dropped my head in disappointment, but outwardly I dared not move. She was using drugs again, and I would be at the mercy of her addiction once more.

"You been acting a fool in school again, haven't you?"

My eyes widened. I couldn't think of a particular incident. Did the teacher call? I wasn't a goody-two-shoes, but I knew that I hadn't done anything that would elicit this type of response from her or a phone call home.

"Motherfucker, I'm talking to you!"

"No ma'am," I answered abruptly.

"You lyin'," God told me that you been in that school acting like a damn fool!"

"No ma'am!" I tried to plead with her. "I ain't do nothing!"

She snatched out her cigarette, leapt from her chair, and stood over me square on.

"You saying God lied on you, nigga?"

What could I say? How could I challenge God? More than likely "God" speaking to her was just a drug-induced hallucination, but I didn't understand that at the time. The use of God's name to cause me harm created a distrust in religion that would follow me into my adult years.

Without hesitation, my mother struck me with a blow to the chest that knocked me to the floor. She hovered over me and followed up with a few more punch/slap combinations, but all I could do was take each hit and wait until she was finished. As much as I wanted to, I couldn't fight her back. It was just something that I refused to do because I was deeply afraid of my mother and what she would do if I did retaliate.

She finally tired herself out and left me alone. The bruises on my body could not compare to the continuous

CHAPTER 1

wounds my mother would inflict on my soul. She was, however, my mother—the person who brought me into the world and tried to care for me to the best of her ability. There was a duty-bound honor that I held for her, despite the constant mental and physical affliction she caused.

* * *

I entered this world in October of 1968 in Detroit, Michigan. According to my late maternal grandmother, mine was a complicated birth. The doctor informed my grandma that either my mother or I wouldn't make it out of the delivery room alive. My mother was losing a lot of blood and I was literally hung inside of her womb by the umbilical cord. At some point, a decision was made for my mom to have a cesarean delivery. By the Almighty's grace and mercy, both my mom and I made it out of that drama with our lives. The tumultuous circumstances of my birth would continue to set the stage for the turmoil that would continue to be a part of my life from then on.

I did not have a Hallmark Channel family awaiting my arrival. Although the blessing of life itself had been bestowed, I had no idea just how many twists, turns, and obstacles awaited me. Most would agree that the safest place a child can be is in the arms of his mother and that the highest form of love that a child would ever experience is the love of their mother. Unfortunately, the hands that were meant to comfort were used to hurt, and the heart that was supposed to love was simply incapable of giving such love.

In my young mind, the dysfunction that I was experiencing while growing up was normal, it was all I knew. I assumed every child experienced the same sort of dysfunction that I had. But why? Why did my mother mistreat me? Did she not want me?

* * *

I wasn't born into wealth or privilege—in fact—most of my life I was steeped in extreme poverty. We moved around a lot, but every house had the uniform mark of a humble lifestyle. The cupboards would usually be rickety and worn down and the dingy, faded wallpaper told a story of neglect and disregard. My mother tried her best to keep the roaches and rats away, but it was their territory just as much as it was ours. Our appliances were worn and low-end, and we had a permanently stained bathtub. In some houses, there were missing doors and makeshift windows—I didn't understand how some of these houses were even inhabitable and how someone was actually charging people to live there. My brother and I often slept on mattresses on the floor—I'm not sure when I finally slept in a bed for the first time. It never dawned on me just how poor we were because everyone around me lived in similar conditions. Sometimes we shared a one-bedroom home and the rooms were divided by a simple sheet. You can imagine the horror that I experienced hearing my mother's intimate encounters with the men she would bring home often.

CHAPTER 1

Sometimes lights went out. Sometimes food was scarce, and sometimes meals were meager. It was a depressing existence for sure, but I'm grateful to the Detroit Focus Hope organization which saved the day many times with that infamous government block cheese. I learned early that cheese, crackers, and a cup of water can stop hunger pains. Our clothes were often second hand and it was rare that I had the luxury of a new pair of shoes or a new—anything.

Many of our misfortunes were directly related to my mother's drug abuse and the psychological battles she faced alongside it. We didn't have much money, but a lot of the money we did have was delegated to my mother's lifestyle. When she was high, her episodes were random, and I never knew what to expect. Walking on eggshells is an understatement—I often felt as though I was walking on hot coals around her. One misstep, one wrong breath—one misunderstanding could land me in the thralls of a severe chastisement.

Despite my tumultuous upbringing, I wasn't a bad kid. In fact, I often dreamt of being a pro boxer or a firefighter. I definitely had the hands to earn a living as a fighter, but it was something about rescuing people from burning buildings that really intrigued me. In some ways, I think that I did become a firefighter—only the people I rescue aren't facing a physical fire: it's a mental one.

* * *

Sometimes, I like to imagine how my mother could have been or who she could have been if not for her own troubled past. I have faint memories of what she looked like when she was healthy and the life that she had inside of her. One of my favorite pictures of my mother showcased the totality of her beauty—it showcased the ghost of a vibrant woman with a full jet black afro, glistening brown skin, a mini skirt, long legs, and an infectious smile. In my earliest recollections of my mother, she would call my brother and me into the living room to dance with her and do the "bump." My favorite times were when she would wake us up in the middle of the night and take us to White Castle. I felt adventurous and a little like a rebel. A little boy my age, up at all hours of the night with a White Castle burger? That was the good life.

I don't believe that people are innately good or bad, but that our circumstances and environment shape who we will ultimately become if we don't make a conscious decision to change—my mother was no exception. She was born and raised in Mississippi in October of 1944. She was one of 13 children and their parents, my grandparents, were sharecroppers. Survival took precedence over education in those days, especially with all those mouths to feed and bodies to clothe. My grandfather decided that everyone should work instead of going to school. Education, I later found out, was very important to my mother but she wasn't allowed to pursue it.

Growing up, my mother knew three things: violence, abuse, and extremely hard work. The environment she

CHAPTER 1

was raised in was wrought with racism, bigotry & male chauvinism. On the one hand, I believe that the childhood my mother experienced, forged her into the headstrong, thick-skinned, brave woman that she was. There wasn't too much of anything that could put fear in her heart. On the other hand, she also developed some very deep and disturbing mental health issues as a result of her childhood traumas. Despite the many stories of bravery and strength I had heard about my grandfather, a darker and more hushed story was how he sexually abused some of his daughters. According to my mother she was among the abused. I believe that the alleged sexual abuse at the hands of her own father, was the foundation of many of my mother's mental health issues.

My mother decided to leave Mississippi, abandoning a husband who, according to most, treated her very well. She was bored and yearned for the excitement of the so-called "big city life" she heard stories of. Unfortunately, she fell into a faster-paced inner-city life than she bargained for. The men in Detroit, Michigan that my mom encountered were of no good character. They were what's referred to as "Jive turkeys," or men who had a "gift of gab" but who were also very broken themselves. My mom fell prey to the slick-tongued, street hustlers of the hood and they played her like a fiddle. As strong as she was, she was also very naïve and easily manipulated. At some point, my mom was persuaded into drug usage. Her experimentation began with pills such as "Dillies" (Dilaudid), "Tees & Blues" (pentazocine and tripelennamine), as well as hallucinogens such as mescaline. Later, her addictions led to heavier and more serious drug use such as "hashish," laced marijuana, as well as "freebase" cocaine among others. It wasn't long before she was persuaded to start selling the con-men's dope for them, all while trying to maintain an addiction of her own and raise two boys. Unfortunately, I'm a witness to the deterioration of my mother's mind and body due to drug use. As a child, I couldn't quite figure it out but I knew my mother was not the same person. She had become very mean and confrontational and was willing to resort to any and all forms of aggression and violence at the drop of a hat.

* * *

My brother and I tried our best to get by, despite my mother, despite our circumstances. He was only a year younger than me, but I felt responsible for him—I even envied him. He didn't have to deal with the physical abuse that my mother inflicted. I was always the object of her violent outbursts. Later, as adults, when my brother and I had a deep conversation about how starkly different our upbringing had been, he reminded me of something I would never forget.

"Dell, you received the abuse, but I had to watch it. What do you think that did to me?"

I had no response. It was one thing for me to endure the physical aspect of our upbringing, but I hadn't thought about how much he also suffered.

CHAPTER 1

As a matter of fact, one time my mother even made my little brother an accomplice to her terror. As usual, I could never really pinpoint when she would explode, but this day, she had something sinister in mind.

"Ma, what we got to eat?" I rummaged through the refrigerator and cabinets after school.

"Oh so you must got a job then, huh?" my mother snapped. "Walking around here like somebody owe your ass. Like I'm supposed to cater to your every got damn need!"

"No ma'am, I'm not saying that!" I tried to clarify. It was too late. She was already convinced that I was disrespectful, ungrateful, and in need of discipline.

"Who the fuck you getting loud with?"

Before I had an opportunity to try to de-escalate the situation, I was blocking punch-kick combinations. I had to be about 10 or 11 at the time, so my mother was much stronger than me. As per usual, she mercilessly wailed on me. Only this time, she mistook my blocking as an attempt to strike her.

"You tryna fight me, muthafucker?!"

She dragged me to one of the mattresses on the floor and pinned me down. She then yelled to my brother, who watched in horror, "Bring me that cord!"

Neither my brother nor I was prepared for what would come next.

"Tie the cord around his neck."

My brother froze. I looked at him, hoping he could feel me begging for him not to comply, but I knew that was useless.

"Nigga, did you hear me? I said tie it around his neck!"

He did what my mother asked, and pulled on the cord which was draped over her bedroom door tighter with her every beckoning. The cord was tied around my neck so tightly that I felt a warm puddle begin to form underneath me. She was deranged for sure, but she told my brother to stop—I guess she had sense enough not to kill me. Relieved, my brother instantly dropped the cord.

"Clean this piss up."

She left the room, and my brother and I cleaned up the mess in silence. I was upset with him for what she made him do, but I knew that he had no choice. Although I resented the preferential treatment my brother received, I always knew that all we really had was each other. Unfortunately for me, this was the type of treatment that had become all too familiar to me. My mother has chased me with knives throughout our small house after getting high several times. Somehow being chased by someone with a knife isn't as traumatic as actually getting caught and that person makes you believe they're going to stab you to death. On one occasion she shot at me in our kitchen with a .22 rifle. I scrambled underneath the kitchen table and curled into a ball so as to make myself as small as possible all while mentally preparing my body for the pain of a bullet. My mother used violence against me as an intimidation factor to maintain control. I think control was very important to her as she failed to control my dad to make him stay with her, and she was losing control over herself through addiction. The worst times were when

CHAPTER 1

she'd be getting high in the dark. I could see the little red tip of the drugs she'd be smoking get brighter as she inhaled while sitting in the darkened front room. After getting high, it was almost certainly going to be "tornado time" over any little thing.

* * *

Throughout these horrendous experiences, I always wondered where my father was. To me, he was just as real as the invisible man. Why wasn't he there to make sure I was safe? Why did he leave me in the hands of a broken woman who, subsequently turned me into a monster? The first time I learned that the man who I thought was my father actually wasn't, I was more confused than ever.

"Hey, Dad," I said to the tall, slim deep brown man sitting beside my mother on the couch." Can I have—."

"Boy, I ain't yo daddy!" he barked back at me. "Girl, what you don' told this boy?" The man cut his glance toward my mother. He cackled a bit and then puffed one more time on his cigarette before he left. I looked to my mother for some type of explanation, but she had nothing to offer. She nonchalantly waltzed past me as if I wasn't a still mass of devastation. If the man I thought was my father was not, then who was?

There were a few men who came in and out of our home, and consequently, my life, who my mother had told me was my father. None of them looked like me, so I suspect my dad didn't stay in our home after my birth for any significant length of time. I don't know if it was because she was manipulating them or using them or what, but I never knew what it was to have a father or father figure. It was an emptiness that I never knew existed until I reached out for a male role model and found there were few to reach back. To this day, I still don't know who my biological father is, and I assume that he's dead by now. My family didn't know who my father was either, and so it got to the point where I just didn't give a damn. As the saying goes, "You can't miss something you never had."

If he is still alive, and I had an opportunity to meet him, I would have a very interesting conversation with him. Would my life have turned out any differently with him in it? I can speculate all day, but the answer could still be no. My mom trusted and dated street dudes who were terrible, so I'd be willing to bet that whoever he is/was, he probably wasn't any different from the rest. Sometimes I wonder if I have other siblings and if so, what kind of cards had life dealt to them? What I am sure of is that he left a bad stain on my mother's heart, and she, in turn, took all that anger and hurt out on me. Whatever he did, it traumatized her to the point that she hated him and it felt like she hated me, too.

Sometimes when I was young, after she'd gone "ham" on me, I can recall thinking, "Me and my dad *must* look alike." She never treated my brother as badly as she treated me. My mother adored my brother's dad, and it showed–she was always affectionate toward him. He and my younger brother

CHAPTER 1

looked like twins. I'm embarrassed to admit it but, although his dad was an alcoholic, I sometimes harbored feelings of envy toward my little brother because his dad—with all of his flaws—was "real and in the flesh." I witnessed on a daily basis just how differently my brother and I were treated growing up. It seemed that in their eyes, my brother could do no wrong. Anything that happened in the household was "Dell's fault." My brother figuratively got away with murder on a daily basis and once he became aware of the power he held, it was used against me at will. I witnessed them coddle and baby my brother well into adulthood, showering him with attention, love, and affection that I never experienced or knew.

CHAPTER 2

How does a young Black boy living in impoverished conditions, suffering from constant abuse, and lacking a father deal with it all? I tried my best to make sense of my life and how things played out, but I didn't know how to manage it all in a healthy way. I was a kid. How could an adult even deal with the hell that was my everyday reality? I became a ball of anger and aggression; while I didn't have the courage to push back and challenge my mother, I had different outlets to do so.

It was hard to escape my mother, but when I did, I was hopeful. Sometimes my favorite uncle used to pick me up to spend the night with him and his kids. I lived for those times. My cousins and I would stay up all night just being kids and doing dumb shit, but it was the home life that I had dreamed about. Normalcy. Love. Safety.

When I didn't spend time with my uncle, my grandmother was my safe place. She had a love that was unmatched. I don't think she ever said a negative word to me, and she was always encouraging and embracing me. I learned later on, however, that she needed me just as much as I needed her. My grandfather, even in his old age, was still an abuser. He would come home drunk and enraged in the middle of the night, and sometimes he would beat my grandmother. The nights that I would stay on the couch, he didn't hit her. Had I known early on that this was happening, I would have stayed on the couch forever.

* * *

I never told anyone about what was happening to me at home, even though there were teachers and other adults who were growing suspicious of me. For better or worse, she was my mother, and I didn't want her to ever be hurt or get into trouble. In my young adolescent mind, she was all that I had. When I was asked about bruises and extension cord marks by teachers or family, I would make up stories so that no one would suspect my mom. I made people think my household was peaceful. I learned how to "fake it" when in actuality I was just trying to get through each day as safely as I could.

Only faking it had its drawbacks. I tried to pretend that nothing was wrong for so long and endured the pain of my afflicted existence for so long that eventually, I stopped talking altogether. I was experiencing some sort of mental breakdown, which I discovered was childhood PTSD. Imagine what it's like being trapped inside of your own mind. You want to scream. You want to tell your abuser to stop. You want someone to come to your rescue, but you know that no one would unless you told them what was wrong. My mind was weary, so I decided to stop all verbal communication for a while.

After a few weeks of having no audible language, I was referred to a mental institution for evaluation, where I lived for a few months. This was my first time being institutionalized, and although I was no longer being abused, it wasn't heaven either. For all intents and purposes, it looked like a prison for kids. The steel gray walls and carpeting had a chilling effect. There was nothing bright, warm, or welcoming about the facility. Everything was stoic and matter-of-fact—from the hallway smells, to the calculated food choices. There was constant EEG testing where staff would attach electrodes to your head to read your brain activity occasionally. I can still sense the cold gel used to secure the electrodes to my scalp. If this was to be a place to make me better, I don't know how they could have achieved it. The staff as well as the environment was both cold and impersonal.

I felt alone and guarded because I was surrounded by strangers who did even stranger things. There was one boy who drew a pentagram on the floor beneath his bunk claiming to have the power to conjure demons. There was another who held full-blown conversations with himself out loud, and he would talk the whole damn day.

"You're going to take your dogs out and go for a walk!"

"No, that doesn't sound like a good idea, Henry!"

CHAPTER 2

"You're an idiot, of course, dogs need to go on walks!"

"Screw you, Henry."

I didn't know what the hell was wrong with Henry, but I knew we couldn't have been there for the same reason. In fact, the more I observed the other kids around me and some of the issues they were playing out, I started to believe that I really didn't belong there. I didn't require psychotropic medications I wasn't a danger to myself or anyone else, and I could function without the assistance of a caregiver. I also knew that I couldn't tell them the truth about what was going on with me.

The staff tried to incorporate a lot of group activities, but I preferred to be alone. I wanted and needed friends, but I wasn't sure who I could trust. There were a few kids who tried to get me to engage, but once they learned that I was unwilling to speak to them, they backed off. I probably came off as weird, and if I was, I was in good company.

I guess being away for a while gave me the mental break that I needed from my mom, so before long, I was back to my old self again. I do feel that in some ways, the individuals responsible for my treatment failed me. They released me back into the same hostile, abusive environment that was responsible for my mental collapse. They didn't investigate my mother or anyone else in my life. Who knows: if they would have pried a little more, maybe I would have told them what was going on. I desperately wanted to, but there is one ghetto rule you never break no matter how young you are: *never* speak about what goes on in your house!

I had made up my mind that I didn't want to go back to the mental institution, but I had to find a way to survive. I had to find a way to channel my pain somewhere else. Violence was so much a part of my daily life that I ended up using it as a coping mechanism outside of my home, too.

Dealing with my mom's abuse was one thing, but when I went to school, I had to deal with bullying from my classmates, too. We were poor, so I came to school with the best that I had—which wasn't that good compared to the other kids. I came into the classroom in my usual hand-me-down off-brand clothes, which made me a prime target for the bullies and class clowns. On top of that, I was a smart kid. I learned quickly that it wasn't "cool" to be smart, so while my teachers praised my work and intelligence, I had to "dumb" myself down so that I could try to fit in.

Unfortunately, my plan didn't work very well as I was bullied and got my ass kicked on a regular basis. I didn't know how to fight at all, and no matter how I tried to throw my hands, I couldn't land a good hit to defend myself well. Once my uncle caught wind of what was going on, he made it his business to teach me how to fight so that I could retain some dignity on the schoolyard.

"You can throw a right hook, but you gotta learn how to get that left jab fist just as powerful cause ya jab will set up everything else dawg," my uncle would instruct me. I took time jabbing him with my left and blocking him with my right, and after a while, I built up my strength and precision. He was my ghetto sensei—my hood Mr. Miagi. He gave me what I needed to feel confident when I went back to school.

One time when I was maybe in 7th or 8th grade, I had the opportunity to showcase all the work I was putting in with my uncle when I had reached my limit for heckling and teasing from my classmates. I walked inside the classroom and they barely gave me enough time to sit down well before they started.

"This nigga look like he need a sign on the freeway!" I heard one of the boys in my class snicker. The class erupted in laughter, and I found myself filling with rage, but mostly embarrassment.

"Fuck you, nigga!" was all I could manage in retaliation. What could I say back? These were some of the freshest, well-put-together boys in the school, and I had nothing to say about them.

The teacher tried her best to diffuse the situation, but she had little influence. She probably didn't even care. I was gaining a sort of negative attitudinal reputation among the staff and teachers, so I'm pretty sure she knew that there was nothing she could do to stop me and that I probably wouldn't be at the school for long anyway.

Later on, when I saw the same group of boys at lunch, I walked by hoping not to be noticed and humiliated by them again. I thought I was in the clear until I heard someone say, "Got any spare change for Spratt?" That was it. Before I could even calculate my next step, my fists were all over one of the boys, and he felt every ounce of my rage. I wasn't just hitting him because of his remarks. I was hitting him thinking about every time I was defenseless against my mother and had to bear her violence. I was hitting him to take back the power that I didn't have inside my own home.

* * *

At this point, my mind was made up. I decided that if someone messed with me, I was going to beat that ass and beat it good. I became a bully and terror upon my peers. I would just wait for someone to oppose me just so I could release some frustration and anger on them. I became proficient at taking lunch money and bus tickets if students received them. I would follow them into the bathroom and demand they "give-'em up or get fucked up!" I was a natural brawler. I didn't win every bout, but I was willing to go to next-level viciousness, so I rarely got a round two. I became very brazen.

My school peers started avoiding me and reporting my negative behavior, so it had gotten tougher to exploit them. I had been kicked out of several different public schools by now due to my behavior, so I figured I had to broaden my field of play. As I got into more trouble, my mother would beat my ass like clockwork, but that wouldn't stop me from wreaking havoc wherever I went.

Because my anger was so potent and so domineering, I seldom had the energy to dig into other emotions and experiences of boys my age. I liked girls a lot. I sure as hell

CHAPTER 2

found many of them attractive, but I was awkward when it came to expressing myself to girls. I think there were a few of them who might've thought I was cute or maybe wanted to get to know me better, but I'm sure to them I seemed intimidating and scary as hell.

There was one girl in my class who was arguably the prettiest girl I had ever seen. She had smooth medium-brown skin, thick, long hair, and gorgeous almond-shaped eyes. What I liked most about her was her body. This was the age when girls started to develop; I liked all of it. One time we were sitting in class, and I noticed that she kept glancing in my direction. A normal dude would have probably smiled at her or sent her a note to ask her to be their girlfriend. Not my ass—I was so paranoid and felt that everyone hated me and had it out for me. I couldn't accept that a girl would like me—especially because I dealt with low self-esteem and never experienced love from my mother. Instead of returning her obliviously flirtatious energy, I snapped at her instead.

"The fuck you looking at?"

Her eyes got bigger and then she made sure that she stopped looking in my direction. Maybe she liked me. Maybe she didn't. If she did like me, I ruined all chances of anything happening between us.

After that, I said to myself, "fuck'em! I'm gonna focus on gettin paid." I recall sitting on my porch one Saturday morning—after yet another school expulsion—when I spotted the newspaper boy on his collection route. He was about my age or maybe a year or so older. I jumped off of the porch, met him halfway up the block (so he wouldn't see my house), and struck up a nonsense conversation with him. He took the bait. I asked if he was collecting and whether he was alone.

He replied, "Yeah. My mom is circling the block for me though."

I thought to myself, "Enough time to rob his ass and get gone."

While he continued to ramble, I hit him in the nose. He quickly grabbed at it with both hands trying to contain the bleeding, and I reached into each of his pockets, cleaning them out. Back then, the folks that received the newspapers used a small manilla envelope to place their collection money into so that the paperboy could pick them up at the end of each week. I ended up with about ten little manilla envelopes full of bills. I felt rich and in total control. I treated all my homeboys to arcade games and smothered hot chili fries. I didn't realize it at the time, but I had adopted the same abusive and violent tactics that my mother used to control me and others. There was a monster created in me that was reckless, and it had a hunger for the street life.

I made the decision to pursue a life much different that yielded better promises than the one that I experienced. The final straw for me was when my mother threw a butcher knife at me and stabbed my penis. By this time, I challenged her more than I did when I was younger—not to much, but I was bolder with my smart-alecky comments. My mother was

CHAPTER 2

standing in the kitchen cutting up chicken when I walked in and asked her for some money.

"Now you know goddamn well I ain't got no money," she responded, still cutting the fresh chicken breast on the glass plate that served as a cutting board. I knew she would say that, but I was still annoyed.

"You got money to get high though," I mumbled and attempted to walk away.

"What the fuck you say, motherfucker?"

Before I could turn around to clean up what I had said, she flung the butcher knife at me and it struck me right in my little dick. I panicked and let out a blood curdling yell while dashing toward the backdoor.

"Come back here, mutherfucker!" my mother screamed as I ran outside of the house with blood dripping down my white Adidas track pants. Out of all the ways she had hurt me in the past, this had to be the worst by far. I must have blacked out because I don't remember how I got back to the house—I just remember her wrapping a cloth around my penis and the blood stains that covered me. She never took me to the hospital. How could she even explain that? CPS would have taken my brother and me out of that house so damn quick if they knew that she stabbed me. I had plans, so I didn't want to end up in the system, and I guess she didn't want me to either. Although I was left with a scar, I healed without any loss of functionality.

All I knew was that I needed to find how to get away from her. By any means necessary.

CHAPTER 3

I often reflect on how I came to live a life filled with bad decisions, criminal activity, and violence. Most children are born with a "blank slate," and gradually make decisions based on their environmental influences. Unfortunately, my slate was dingy from the start. Drugs and crime were always a part of my home, and nobody tried to shield me from it. My mother sold hashish and other drugs, and I started to observe how the people around me operated. By the time I was six years old, I had a "fuck the police" mentality and was being indoctrinated by criminals.

The one person I really looked up to and admired was one of my mother's siblings. Since I didn't have a father figure consistently around, he was the closest thing to a father that I had. My uncle was a real "street dude." We are a little closer in age, so naturally, folks in the hood thought we were brothers. I really admired how he navigated both people and the hustle game. He would mesmerize me with

CHAPTER 3

stories of shoot-outs and brushes with death and the law. My uncle knew all of the hood movers and shakers and they respected him as well. He hustled and made plenty of money. Unk had women, cars, and clothes so who better to emulate?

By the time I was about 13 years old, I'd do my best to be around him every chance I could. Although at first he didn't like it, I followed him around all the time and always visited the corners where he sold drugs. I was always fascinated by the loud hip-hop music glaring out of the old school rides, the beautiful females hanging around the crew, the flashy clothes and jewelry as well. One day he told me, "If you're going to be coming up here all the time, you might as well be the look-out." I was tasked with alerting him and the rest of the crew if I saw something fishy going on or if I spotted the "one time" (police) lurking too close to the "spot", slang for the street corners they controlled. In exchange for my services, they would pay me in brown grocery bags full of coins. After I would count up all of my earnings, I realized that some of the bags would have between five hundred to a thousand dollars worth of change.

I had been street hustlin' for nearly a year, and the money I was earning gave me a sense of euphoria. I was able to not only stay fresh with the latest clothes but to put food on the table at home, as well. I was able to pay off the party store credit tab that my mom had accrued as well. I wanted to earn more on a larger scale though, so I asked my uncle to school me on the street game. Instead, he sat me down and explained why he didn't want me in it. What Unk wanted initially was for me to keep my little punk-ass in school. Oftentimes we don't realize it but most of the folk around us want the best for us, even if they aren't exercising wisdom for themselves. They're very aware of the price we'll have to pay for wrong choices because they have bumped their own heads and survived on the road of folly.

At this time, I was about fourteen and had already decided that I didn't need advice from anybody. My mind was made up. I wanted to make my own bones—to be my own man, or what I thought was a man. I met a couple of dudes from West Warren & 14th. Street while scarcely attending Murray Wright H.S. and we became thick as thieves very quickly. I used to run the streets with them all the time, doing petty crimes and trying to prove to them that I was just as "thugged-out" as they were. In my attempts to be accepted by my new crew, I decided to go along with them to break into a house. Up until this point, I hadn't imagined doing anything like this before. Sure, robbing the paperboy for a few dollars or being the "lookout" for the dope boys was nothing for me, but entering somebody's home was an entirely different level. Nonetheless, I listened intently as they laid out the plan for this heist and what my role would be.

"Alright, Tone, you gon' be the lookout," Mike, who fashioned himself as the leader of our crew, instructed.

"Cool," Tone complied.

"Dell, you're the smallest, so you gon' be the one to go in the window and grab the shit."

CHAPTER 3

"Aight," I agreed. I wasn't scared, but I did want to make sure that I wouldn't be caught up in some bullshit because of them. So many questions rushed my thoughts, but I knew if I asked too many, it would seem like I was afraid. I needed to know how long I should be in there and what exactly was I going to take. What if they didn't have anything valuable? Shit, what if they had a dog or a shotgun? I resolved to just wait for the play-by-play and do exactly what they told me to do.

Once Mike told us which house, we would rob and which day we would do it, everything was in place, and it was just up to me to do my part. We rode a rickety dark-blue van—one that we had stolen earlier— to the victim's house at about two in the morning. *Was anybody home?* I thought to myself. I assumed that people would be at home nestled in their beds around this time, and I didn't understand how we would be able to rob people while they were home.

"Yo, what if somebody's in there?" I finally gathered my nerve and asked.

"Ain't nobody in there, lil' nigga," Mike confirmed. I was running down all the possible scenarios and all the possible ways that this could go wrong in my mind but dared not utter them.

I was anxious to show them that I was just as much of a dog as they were. I was totally committed to the task. I followed some of the other guys in the crew around to the back of the house, and I waited intensely for Mike to pop open the window. Once Mike succeeded, they lifted me up, and I wiggled my way into what looked to be someone's bedroom. There was no rhyme or reason to the house, just a lot of stuff everywhere. It looked like whoever lived there had probably robbed other people and stored their spoils inside the house. Maybe we were robbing other thieves. The irony.

I didn't spend too much time gawking. I started to grab speakers, VCRs, and other electronics and funneled them out the window to Mike.

"Check the drawers to see if they got cash!" Mike loudly whispered to me from below. I was ready to get the hell out of there and now he wanted me to look for *more* stuff? Like an obedient soldier, I rummaged through closets and drawers and found two stacks of money hidden behind some bundled-up grocery bags. *Hell yea,* I thought to myself. I slipped the money into my pockets and slipped back out of the window like a wet seal.

"Alright, let's get the fuck out of here!" Mike ran towards the van, where Tone was keeping watch. I was right on his heels and damn-near flew into the van. Tone scurried off and we made it back to our "hideout" without incident.

After we loaded all of our stolen merchandise into the house and took "inventory," Mike asked me if I had found any cash or dope before I came back out. I didn't want to tell him about the cash, and I figured that he wouldn't know if I kept it for myself because I deserved a whole stack! I took all of the mother fucking risks while they were outside waiting.

CHAPTER 3

Then I thought that I should give him one stack and keep the other.

Mike took the money, smiled, and said, "Damn, little nigga, you cleaned up!"

I smirked and tried to play cool, but I was still trembling from the rush of it all. I never liked the home invasion game but, when in Rome—

At some point, I progressed from petty thievery to an "enforcer" for the local dope dealers. I guess it was a natural progression because I had a little size on me for my age, I liked to fight, and I was wild. A few times, drug lieutenants in the hood would hire me to wreck one or two of their workers who might've messed up some money or dope or both. They'd pay me nice cash to wear a mask and a pair of leather gloves and whoop some ass—easy money. One time, I had to pay a visit to a husband and wife duo and beat both their asses. They were a pair of addicts who received dope in exchange for letting drug dealers sell dope out their home. Between the husband, wife, and the young dope pusher who was staying there, the product mysteriously came up short. I didn't feel so bad about whooping the husband's ass, but I was convicted in my soul about hitting the wife. Prior to this, I had never hit a woman, and I had reservations about hitting her. Although I had to go through with it, when it came to the woman, I consciously pulled my punches. It was enough to fool my benefactor. I realized I was hired to do a job and failing to do so would have resulted in my ass being buried in the backyard.

After we robbed a couple more houses, and I had beaten a few more asses, I had proven myself to Mike and the rest of the crew. They noticed I possessed both heart and hustle, so they introduced me to their heroin connection. The rest was history. We began selling dope together as a crew. Not only did we sell heroin, but we also mixed, sifted, packed, and bundled it. I eventually told my uncle what I was doing, and he decided that if I was going to be immersed in the drug world, he would teach me the portion of the game I was lacking. He also felt it wise to hustle with guys from my own hood. I got introduced to a couple of the "Big Dogs" from my neighborhood who were strong in the game and making shit happen. I quickly built relationships with them and one of them eventually fronted me with some heroin tester bundles to give away. I literally gave out free dope samples to the addicts so as to draw in new "customers" to my "product" and ultimately establish my own dope spot or corner.

Back then, a heroin bundle consisted of 12 packets of "mix jive," heroin mixed with quinine and lactose. Each packet sold for $12 apiece, so the most that a bundle would fetch was $144. One hundred went back to the "connect," or the person who fronted me the drugs, and the remaining $44 was my profit. My goal was to pass out the free mix jive blows to the addicts in hopes that they'd leave their current dealer and do exclusive business with me. It was like running a corporate operation: there were inventory checks, and profit margins to meet. I needed to get my

CHAPTER 3

"spot" pumping somewhere between 200 and 300 bundles of mix jive a day.

It would be a shame for a customer to overdose on some of your products, but at the same time, you'd become an automatic hit if it happened. The word on the streets would be that you have an "O.D. blow" (or a product so good that people would risk overdose) and they'd be knocking down your door to get it. As a dealer, that was the status one strives to obtain and maintain. I know it sounds cruel. Someone overdosing means they could die, but this was the game and that was the product. The drug game is the business of human exploitation, plain and simple. Money is always the endgame, not people. I was caught up, and as the saying goes, "All drug sellers aren't bad people, but bad people sell drugs." I was struggling to figure out where I fell on the spectrum.

I was about fifteen years old when I started selling my dope in a local "hit house." A hit house is usually an abandoned and dilapidated house, hotel, or apartment building that usually reeks of feces, urine, and all manner of human filth. There would be addicts lying everywhere with needles sticking out of any place that a live vein could be accessed: thighs, necks, arms, webs of toes, and sometimes vaginas. As the person working the hit house, I lived there, too, because, keep in mind, the goal was to always meet the customer's demand or someone else would. Hit houses always ran the risk of getting raided by law enforcement at any time. They could also be invaded by a rival crew who would "stomp" you and take your product, or you could even lose your life over it. The addicts didn't have an allegiance to anyone or anything except their habits so they would sell your ass out quickly to the person with the biggest dope offer. Because of those odds, I decided to get some protection. I bought my first throw-away gun—a rusty midnight special .38 caliber, five-shot revolver.

* * *

Despite mostly living in the hit house, I was back and forth to my mother's house, checking on my brother and keeping up with my friends in the neighborhood. Although I was running my own small drug operation, I was still a minor, and I still needed parental intervention for some things.

My mother hadn't changed much. She was still as wild, violent, and unpredictable as ever, and at some point, I had even become numb to her threats and outbursts. The last time my mother actually hit me was definitely an awakening moment for both of us. I seldom remember what triggered her when she would beat me, but as always, she was high. This time, she was beating me with a braided extension cord, but I refused to cry. It's not that I didn't physically register the pain of the event, I just refused to cry anymore. What was the point? She wouldn't stop if I did. I wouldn't learn whatever lesson I was supposed to learn from the beating. She would just do it again for any random reason, and no one would be there to help me.

She snarled and angrily asked, "Boy you ain't crying?"

CHAPTER 3

I defiantly answered, "Nope!"

It was at that moment I believe she realized that shit was different now. She couldn't do any more damage that hadn't already been done. I'd been broken and rebuilt into an emotional ice box. Was that her intention all along? I don't believe it was, but I was morphing into someone that neither she nor I could imagine I would become.

CHAPTER 4

By the time I turned 16, I started to make a name for myself on the block. I was making a consistent income selling drugs—I earned the respect of my peers and old heads who had been in the game longer than me. This new lifestyle opened a whole new world of opportunities for me. Whenever I did decide to make an appearance at school, I made sure that I was dressed in the latest name brands and would buy the most expensive shit my money could get. I was arrogant and full of myself. My confidence was through the roof, and I felt like I was invincible.

Feeling more confident than ever, I even tried my luck in the romance department. I pretended to be more than I was and let the materialistic things that I had speak for me. Even though I was "the man" I was still awkward when it came to girls. I had seen my uncle and the other guys I admired rotate women like they rotated shoes; it seemed

CHAPTER 4

like the ideal lifestyle, but I didn't think the player lifestyle was for me. Besides, I had never seen a healthy relationship dynamic between a man and a woman. Being deprived so long of love and affection from my mother, I wasn't sure how to give or receive love in return.

My first real girlfriend was someone I knew from the neighborhood. One of my boys introduced us, and it wasn't long before we started to hang out. Prior to her, I was a virgin. I had a tough exterior, but like most boys my age, I was largely intimidated but very excited by the whole idea of sex. The first time I had sex with my girlfriend wasn't anything to write home about—it was over so quick that I hardly remember most of the experience. I also recall how we couldn't go to very many places because of our ages, and I didn't feel comfortable with the idea of taking her to my house because she lived in a nice middle classed neighborhood and I didn't so i was embarrassed. I recall how we'd mostly hang out at the mall traveling by way of the bus or Checker Cab.

I remember the time I decided to surprise my girlfriend with a date to the movies, which turned out to be one of the worst nights of my life. We were coming out of the Norwest Movie Theater on Grand River after seeing *The Last Dragon* and *Fast Forward* when a group of guys decided they would rob me. We were heading toward the bus stop when they approached us.

"Aye, man, those Adidas out cold!" one of the guys approached me. I could tell that something was off about the situation. I was always alert and aware of my surroundings in case a rival tried to catch me slippin'. One of the cardinal rules of the streets is: "keep ya head on a swivel at all times". Although dude complimented my shoes, what he was really saying is that they'd look better on his feet. I was ready for whatever they planned.

Before I could respond, one of the guys tried to mace me in the eyes. I ducked and although some of the substance got on me, It didn't get into my eyes. I quickly pulled out my .38 pistol, and they started running as soon as they saw the gun. That wasn't enough for me though. Their running was like fuel to a fire. I was primitive and animalistic—I had the same drive as a lion who was chasing a gazelle. I wanted them to know that they had fucked up, so I ran to the side of the theater and let off two shots—blam! blam! The bullets missed their marks, but what I didn't know was that one of the theater's ushers witnessed the entire event and had called the police.

"What the fuck are you doing?" my girlfriend panicked.

"C'mon, we gotta get the fuck outta here!"

I pulled her arm, and we bolted up Grand River attempting to get as far away from the scene as possible. I threw the gun into an empty field, and kept running, but then I circled back to retrieve it. That gun was my power and authority. It's strange how an instrument of violence could also offer peace of mind. It made me feared and respected, so how could I part with it? I was bonded to a weapon because I wasn't sure who I was without it.

CHAPTER 4

Unfortunately for us, we weren't fast enough, and a squad car pulled up right beside us. Both officers jumped out and began questioning me.

"Did you see someone fire a gun about 10 minutes ago?" one of them began interrogating.

"I don't know," I lied.

"Someone called in a shooting and said that the subject fit your description."

"I don't know why they would say that. It wasn't me!"

"It wasn't?" the second officer chimed in, clearly agitated by my elusive answers. Then he turned to my girlfriend and questioned her, "Did you or him shoot at somebody? Do you have a gun?"

She was becoming more and more flustered, and I knew that if they questioned her any longer, she would have snitched. She kept her cool though and didn't give them any answers. Eventually, the officers got tired of me lying and evading their questions, and they decided to frisk me.

Oh shit, I thought. I knew that everything would be over at that point.

They found the gun in my right hand, which was wrapped with my Adidas windbreaker jacket.

"Drop your weapon and put your fucking hands behind your back!" the first officer commanded me.

"Please don't arrest him!" I heard my girlfriend squeal. "He didn't hurt anybody!"

The officers called for backup and put us both in two separate cars. I'm not sure where they took her, but they took me to the youth detention center in Downtown Detroit and placed on 6-N, the housing unit for incorrigible male youths with serious charges. When I arrived, I noticed how eerily similar the youth home was to the mental facility where I lived years before. I guess whether you're a mental patient or a criminal, it's little difference in how you're treated—especially if you're Black.

I was charged with carrying a concealed weapon (CCW) and trespassing. Once I appeared in front of the referee, or acting judge, my charges were modified. The CCW was changed to Minor in Possession and the trespassing charge was dropped. I remained in the youth center for about three months and was given a two-year probation stipulation as well.

Shortly after I was released from the youth home, my mother had moved again, and though I didn't want to live with her, my probation gave me no choice. I didn't know who I was supposed to check in with and what the process was to transfer my case, and nobody was looking for me. I got off probation early, which in my case, was not a good thing.

I tried to keep my nose clean for a while, but I was right back into the drug game because it was the only way that I knew to take care of myself. The second thing that I realized was that I needed another pistol, pronto! If I didn't protect me, who would? The streets are cold, so to survive them you had better become a glacier. I tried to resume my relationship with my girlfriend, but that night at the movies

CHAPTER 4

freaked her out so badly that she didn't want anything to do with me after that. I didn't blame her. This wasn't the life for her, but I didn't value our relationship enough to choose her instead.

At this point, I had been involved in shootouts and had been shot as well. I had become more brutal, reckless, and callous, and my sole purpose in life was to get money and survive. I rarely had time for leisure, and there weren't many moments when I could just enjoy life and exhale. I was always looking over my shoulder. Always on the defense. There was a time that I had to jump out of a window on the 2nd floor at the 20 Grand Motel on 14th and West Warren Ave. Some old head hustlers found out that there were some young punks in one of the rooms selling heroin, and they decided to rob our young asses. I was in the room by myself that day. Two old heads bum-rushed me with pistols in hand, forcing me back into the room. They demanded the dope and money. What they didn't know was that our supplier had just left the room about 45 minutes earlier after collecting nearly seventy-five hundred dollars from us. She was scheduled to drop off a fresh "sack" of dope in 2 hours. I just kept yelling to them, "Ain't no money or dope here man! We ain't selling no dope!" After maybe 30 minutes of slapping me around, one of the old dudes went over to the T.V. and turned the volume high. I felt that same familiar chill go down my spine that I felt just before my mother would inflict violence upon me. I had a decision to make and fast so, I made a mad dash off of the bed where they had me seated toward the vertical rectangular glass next to the door of the room. I remember my face hit the glass hard, then I felt the blow of the 2nd story balcony railing hit my midsection as I flipped over it landing squarely on my back, knocking all of the wind outta my lungs. I escaped with my life that day. Believe it or not, that still didn't stop me from running those streets.

***

At the height of my time in the drug game, more money came with even more enemies. Sometimes those enemies came as a result of territory issues, and at other times, my blatant arrogance and disrespect created other enemies. When I was about 17, I began a feud with another group of dealers over some drugs that I was fronted on consignment. The street rule is if you get a "sack" on consignment, get that money and pay the benefactor back immediately. I decided, "Fuck it! Let'em get it like Caesar got Rome!" In a nutshell, I was being an asshole, and I had no intentions of paying them. One night I was getting off the bus heading home from hanging around the "stash" house on Wabash and West Warren Ave., when a few dudes cornered me at the park.

"Yea, that's that nigga that got our shit," one of them pointed out.

"Get the fuck on," I tried to warn them. Only I was outnumbered, and I knew that things would not end well for me. I didn't have my pistol on me either, so I knew that I'd have to fight for my life. I was energized on 51's—a mixture of crack cocaine and marijuana which is smoked like a joint. It was a highly addictive combination introduced to me by my own uncle just a year and a half earlier. I had several near-death experiences where I barely escaped with my life, so I was high and prepared to die that night. But if I was to die, I wasn't going to go out like a punk, so I swung at whoever was closest as the rest of them started beating my ass.

It was brutal. One of them hit me in my temple with a hammer, and I had a knot that swelled up as big as a ping-pong ball. My face was bloody and bruised, and my body ached from all the kicks and punches I endured. I hated that feeling of helplessness and vulnerability. I hated that I was defenseless and powerless—essentially a victim. I decided that I was going to be packing all of the time from that day forward. I was never going to be caught slipping like that again. The streets don't play fair so why should I? The next time something jumped, I wanted to be ready.

For the next three days, thoughts of revenge circulated in my mind and took over my life. I was filled with rage, and the humiliation of that night didn't escape me. It was a particularly hot and humid summer day—the appropriate weather to reflect how much my blood boiled and how my emotions were steaming. After seeing the condition my body was in after the brutal beat-down at the park, it wasn't too difficult convincing my uncle to drive me around the hood. We surveilled the neighborhood as well as the playground where I got jumped, hoping to run into them again. They were a close-knit crew, so I knew that if I saw one, a few others wouldn't be far away; I was banking on them all being together so I could deal with them collectively.

As much as my uncle and I combed that area, we didn't find any of the guys who jumped me, but on June 7, 1987, we did run into someone who was associated with them. He was slightly older than me and lived in my hood, but we weren't well acquainted because we ran in different circles. I had no conflict with him, but as the car pulled up to the intersection, I looked out of my passenger side window and that's when, he began to taunt me about what had happened to me on the playground a few nights prior.

"Yea, I see you got dat ass beat," he laughed. "Don't play with niggas' money."

The embarrassment was overwhelming. I thought about how I felt when the kids at school would bully me and make me feel like shit; I thought about being brutalized by my own mother and hearing her tell me how I wasn't shit. I was so tired of people forming narratives about me that I fought so hard to live beyond. His taunting and teasing were the triggers that unleashed the most horrendous aspect of myself. I thought I had something to prove, but I didn't. The reality is that I was still a scared little boy who played at being a thug. I was hell-bent on proving myself to my uncle, my homeboys, and my hood.

We exchanged more words back and forth. Acting on pure impulse and emotion, I hopped out of my uncle's car, raised my gun, and pulled the trigger. He was hit and now lying on the ground in front of me. In an instant, my future flashed before my eyes, and it was pitch black.

A man lost his life because of my misguided, impulsive, and out-of-control younger self. There's absolutely *nothing* I can either say or do that can undo or change the past, but I believe that the Most-High God has forgiven me. Just as importantly, I've now forgiven myself. I pray that someday the family can find it within their hearts to forgive me as well.

CHAPTER 5

By now there was an All-Points Bulletin for my arrest. I tried to hide out for a few days, but it wasn't long after the fateful incident that the Detroit Police Homicide Division discovered my whereabouts. I went over to one of my homeboy's house near Dexter Ave. to clear my mind and get some advice. We were sitting on the porch and saw my uncle walking up the street. He stopped and said "Whatupdoe?!" to me and my homeboy. "What up Unk?!", I replied. He began to tell me that the homicide detective at 1300 Beaubien Blvd. wanted me to turn myself in for questioning while handing me the detective's business card.

"I have absolutely no plans to talk to any of those mother fuckers!" I recoiled at the thought.

My uncle simply said, "I hear ya nephew...well, I'm out." Then he walked off heading toward Grand River Ave.

I thought to myself, "that was strange".

CHAPTER 5

The detectives not only found out I had a pregnant girlfriend but her identity as well. They "tailed" her until she finally led them to my mother's house where I was taking refuge. When my pregnant girlfriend came over that particular night something felt "off". It felt as though the walls were closing in all around me. Although my girlfriend wasn't "showing" at that point, I was the one experiencing nausea and dizziness. I'm going to jail for the rest of my life, I kept thinking. The torture of waiting to be arrested was almost too unbearable, and for a split-second, I almost thought about turning myself in just to get it over with like my uncle had suggested.

Very early the following morning while everyone was still lying in their beds, from out of nowhere, it seemed all hell had broken loose. An angry male's voice infiltrated the house booming loudly on a bullhorn yelling, "Come out with your hands raised or we're coming in to get your ass!"

I bolted out of bed and ran to the back window to see several officers outside. I couldn't hide any longer. My hands were shaking relentlessly as I attempted to throw on a t-shirt and shorts to figure out a way out of the situation. After getting dressed and realizing I had nowhere to run, I hugged and apologized to both my mother and little brother. I told my pregnant girlfriend I was sorry, took a long deep breath, then walked outside with my hands raised. Once on the porch, I counted no less than six gun barrels pointing at my seventeen-year-old head. Needless to say, I was terrified! I was cuffed, placed under arrest, then tossed in the back of a squad car.

Originally, I received a charge of first-degree homicide (which carried a sentence of "natural life" without parole) as well as a felony firearms charge. Although I was 17 and a half, I was "bound over" on the charges as an adult. I was held in the Wayne County Jail and the legal process took nearly a year. During that year, my anxiety was through the roof. This wasn't like any other institution I had been accustomed to—I figured this was the preface for the rest of my life. While I was still in the Wayne County Jail (WCJ) awaiting my fate, my girlfriend gave birth to my beautiful son in December 1987. It finally dawned on me that I didn't take my unborn child into consideration at all before allowing both anger and impulsivity to get the best of me.

While sitting in the WCJ and being ushered through a process I had absolutely no clue about, I made a spiritual decision. I was determined to be in my son's life no matter what! Despite my situation, I refused to be labeled a deadbeat dad. I was already a better man than whomever my father was because I intended to raise my son. Even behind bars, my son knew who his father was. I was present in his mind and remained in contact with him whenever my mom had a working landline or a valid address.

* * *

I decided to waive my right to a jury trial (after being coerced by the court-appointed lawyer). This meant only the judge would decide my fate by bench trial instead of a jury of my peers. My lawyer convinced me that a bench trial was the better option.

CHAPTER 5

He said that if I took a jury trial and lost, it would cost the State much more money, and the prosecution would've argued for a sentence of "life" or as close to it as possible.

The trial was open and shut. The prosecution sang songs of my violent past and alleged illegal drug activity. They presented this type of evidence and that type of evidence—they painted me as a cancer to society as well as my community. *Maybe I was,* I thought to myself. Maybe prison or a pine box was where I needed to be and where I would have ended up all along. I had feelings of regret and remorse for taking a person's life, and although a willing participant, I also felt bad for my uncle.

After the trial process, I was found guilty of 2nd Degree homicide and Felony Firearm. I received a sentence of 16 to 30 years for the homicide which meant I would spend a minimum of 16 years and a maximum of 30 years in prison. I also received a mandatory two-year sentence for the felony firearm conviction. I had to complete the two-year gun sentence before I even started the 16 to 30-year sentence for the homicide charge.

I could not fathom what 30 years in prison would be like. Hell, being anywhere for 30 years was inconceivable, and to live that long behind bars seemed like the sickest and cruelest punishment to ever assign to someone. But this was the beginning of my reality. Although I was a juvenile, I had to grow up quickly because prison life has no respect for age, race, size, or toughness. It eats the weak as well as the strong. It spits out the remains daily. Like most young folks, I didn't think about the consequences of my actions until it was too late. All those years of abuse, anger, and bullying manifested into one of the single worst decisions I could have ever made. Not only did a man lose his life, but two separate families were left grieving a loved one. What did I gain from my impulsivity? Maybe, I thought it would make others respect me or even fear me. Either way, it didn't matter. I became just another statistic within the so-called "justice system." No longer a young man nor even considered a human being any longer. I allowed my identity to be reduced to a six-digit prison number.

During the long, cold ride on the prison transfer bus, I was hit with an icy cold wave of fear which ultimately gave way to red-hot anger that raced through my entire being. I became enraged at the things and opportunities I had foolishly deprived myself of. Why didn't I finish school? I should've been there to co-parent my child. I realized I would miss so many important steppingstones in my son's life, and it hurt badly. I began regretting not having a healthier relationship with my mother and not being a better influence on my younger brother. I regretted the life that I had chosen. The ugly truth is I realized that I had made a choice to cease living and to merely exist. I began to despise myself.

I had unwittingly become the slave or indentured servant mentioned in the 13th amendment of the constitution. Sadly, this would be my identity for many years to come.

* * *

CHAPTER 5

After being transferred from the WCJ into the MDOC, I had to undergo the Michigan prison quarantine process at the Riverside Correctional Facility (RCF)—a detention center in Ionia, MI designed for youthful offenders. The quarantine process allows the prison administration to screen and classify prisoners to determine their custody and security levels and the specific prison he/she will begin serving their sentence(s). The Michigan Dept. Of Correction (MDOC) security custody levels range from levels 1 through 6. The higher the security level the more restrictive the prison setting is.

I came to RCF with a survivor's mentality. Despite every emotion I was experiencing at the time, as always, anger was the one that always dominated. No matter how afraid I was, fear had no place. I was an asshole. I got into fights with different inmates, and I was defiant and aggressive with corrections officers. I had no idea what to expect from people within RCF, so I made it my business to be the hardest most aggressive inmate in the facility, or as close as possible to it.

While still housed at RCF, I screened as a level 4 security custody. I had accumulated over 35 negative behavior points, which was the maximum an inmate could receive. As a result of my crime and the points I had racked up, I was ultimately transferred to the Michigan Reformatory (MR), infamously known as the "Gladiator School" in Ionia, MI. The Gladiator School was designed specifically for the worst of the worst male offenders under the age of 21. Sadly, the staff seemed to push that very negative narrative versus encouraging positive change in the minds of impressionable youth such as myself.

A day inside of the Reformatory consisted of pooping, pissing, fighting, eating, sleeping, showering, weightlifting—then, rinse and repeat. The staff didn't give a damn about the inmates or our well-being. Their only concern was making sure we were always secured within the walls of the prison. The Reformatory was full of ignorant and impulse-driven young dudes such as myself, but I was fortunate enough to have a few older homies from my neighborhood there who took me under their wing and taught me the 101's of prison survival. If followed, your odds of survival increase significantly. They gave me the top five "no-no's" of penitentiary which were:

1. Steer clear of homosexuals/homosexuality if that wasn't your thing. This one was definitely the easiest to follow.
2. Don't fraternize with the female staff, no matter how flirtatious they were. "Loose" female staff were the cause of several inmate casualties due to jealousy.
3. Stay away from drugs and prison dealers (self-explanatory).
4. Stay off of the basketball court unless you're playing with dudes that you knew from "the streets."
5. Stay away from the gambling tables.

CHAPTER 5

Though they are all terrible situations to find oneself caught up in, gambling boasts the most prison injuries and deaths. On any given prison yard, you'll find sitting tables, which are always situated in the same proximity, a few feet apart. Each table has four steel seats affixed. Most of the tables were unofficially designated gambling tables by the inmates. The remaining tables were left for the spades, checkers, and chess players like myself. I, unfortunately, had a front-row seat to the carnage instigated by gambling. Guys would get their skulls split wide open with a lock in a sock, their throats cut with a razor, or even have an eye stabbed with a homemade ice pick while sitting at the gambling tables. Most of this would happen when they attempted a con called "playing on ass." In this foolish situation, there would be an inmate sitting at the table gambling, but he wouldn't have any money or collateral yet, hoping to win everyone else's money without being exposed as a fraud. Of course, this had severe as well as deadly consequences.

Those five "penitentiary rules" stayed with me for the duration of my sentence. Despite my adherence to them, I still managed to get myself into a lot of trouble with other inmates and staff.

* * *

Because I was still a "fish" (prison yard slang for a newcomer), there were inmates who tried to take advantage of me. I remember an incident that jumped off maybe two months after I arrived at the Reformatory. I didn't have a TV or any of the other luxuries that the other inmates had, so I suppose I was an easy target. One of the biggest complaints I had about the Reformatory was the fact that it was supposed to be a facility for young offenders, yet it still housed older offenders who had no other place to go. That was a disastrous combination: mixing impressionable and vulnerable young men with manipulative and predatory seasoned men. I was a target and was on my way to lunch (or chow) when I was approached by an "old head," or an older inmate.

"Hey young blood, I want you to take this sack down to cell #D5 to my mans, Speedy."

"Shit, alright, that's cool," I agreed not knowing what the hell I was getting myself into.

"All you have to do is drop it off at his bars and then I'll take care of the rest."

It sounded alright to me. I followed the old head's instructions and then went back to my cell.

Later that night, I overheard a conversation between the old head and another inmate, and it sounded like they were talking about me. I felt a chill go up my neck, and I knew something was off about the situation.

"Where is the rest of my money?" I heard an inmate yell, agitated. "It's some shit missing out that sack you sent me dawg."

"I ain't took shit outta ya shit man!" a voice responded. "You betta holla at that fish—he probably took ya shit out ya sack bro!"

CHAPTER 5

I quickly figured out the game: the old head didn't pay the other inmate what he owed him. Instead of owning up to the issue or attempting to escape whatever consequence came along with owing the money, he set me up to take the fall. It would have been nothing to kill me. Though I knew people there, I hadn't established any deep relationships or alliances that would warrant someone going to war alongside me. I was on my own.

I quickly figured out who the "old head" was talking to that night, because the next morning, I had an inmate swinging a homemade knife (fashioned out of a razor blade melted onto a toothbrush) at me full force. He cut me twice before slipping on droplets of my blood. The makeshift knife slid out of his hand as he tried to break his fall, and I moved quickly to kick it under the bars of an unoccupied cell. Now I had a fighter's chance of survival–and I fought hard. We threw fists until the inmate janitor reasoned with us to "let it go" before the Corrections officers came back and we'd be placed in Administrative segregation. We were both exhausted at that point, so we made a b-line back to our individual cells to tend to our wounds. The fact that I didn't snitch on the dude, even though he tried to kill me, coupled with the fact I beat his ass, earned me some respect amongst the other inmates. It made things a little easier for me, but I wouldn't dare say that my time there was easy by a long shot.

As time progressed, different inmates invited me to join their organizations. As much as I wanted to be a loner,

I learned that nobody could survive within the "belly of the beast" without an alliance or two. Even if it appeared an inmate walked the yard by themselves, it was almost certain that they weren't alone.

Prison exposed me to some of the vilest and evil circumstances ever imaginable. If you've never been to prison, you wouldn't believe all the things that can happen inside of any given facility at any given time. I've seen seemingly tough guys become reduced to an even tougher guy's girlfriend. I've seen gang fights, shady staff, crackheads, heroin overdoses, and kingpins who lived like kings. Things that people assume were only happening on the streets was going on within the prison system as well. My goal was strictly survival. Before, I contemplated how I could last 30 years inside of a level 4 prison, but soon my goal was just to last until the next day—and then the day thereafter.

CHAPTER 6

Although prison was full of psychopaths and sociopaths who live for the drama, there were also others who had the heart to educate and empower. I didn't realize how stupid I was until I had men around me educating and correcting my speech and mentality. Even though I was using the word "nigga" frequently with my friends and guys on the streets, I was warned by an old head that "nigga" was a forbidden word in prison.

"If you ever say 'nigga' to somebody in here," the old head began, "You getting stabbed as soon as the doors pop open."

The young, brazen, hot-headed version of myself came to the surface and challenged him. "What? How the fuck you gon' tell me what I can and can't say!"

"Young blood, I'm trying to save your life. You use that word up in here and you'll be dead. I been here a dime and I don' seen shit you ain't never seen."

He could tell that I wasn't convinced, but still, he didn't let me off the hook. "The reason why you use that word and all the other cuss words you say is because you don't have a vocabulary. Go and pick up the dictionary and find out the meaning of the words that you speak."

There were other old heads trying to school me, but it was so hard to receive from them. They were black men attempting to father me, and I consciously resented them for it. They represented the father that I never had, and they triggered the constant feelings of abandonment, rejection, and lack of identity I experienced as a little boy who needed a father.

Nonetheless, they didn't give up on the young, headstrong newbie. I eventually began to apply some of their wisdom. They helped me reshape my thinking and change my outlook on a lot of things. One old head taught me the importance of appearance despite the circumstances. He encouraged me to keep both my black state belt and black state issue boots "spit shined" as well as to keep my shirt neatly tucked into my pants. "Even though you're in here, you still present yourself well," he would always say.

Prior to coming to prison, I had dropped out of school. The importance of education was something that the old heads had renewed within me as well.

"Hey, Youngblood, you finished school out there?"

I replied, "Nope."

"Go over to the schoolhouse and sign up for GED classes, Youngblood!"

CHAPTER 6

It sounded more like an order than a request. I thought I was tough, but it was obvious that those old dudes carried more weight! The command to go to school was something that I followed, and as a result, I earned my GED. I was truly proud of myself for the first time in my life.

Chess was something I never considered playing before, but there I was abandoning the basketball court to watch the old heads strategically move queens, knights, and pawns. I didn't know it then, but they were trying to keep me out of trouble. As much as I tried to resist them and turn a deaf ear, I couldn't help but absorb the wisdom they imparted. Who knows, maybe it was God trying to shield me from negative influences and situations.

The men who mentored me during my time at the Michigan Reformatory were rare, and I dare say that they don't exist in today's prison culture. Most of the old heads today are just as ignorant and destructive as the younger ones, and it's a shame that they don't have the same pride and concern for the well-being of younger generations.

* * *

Over the next few years, I became a sponge, soaking up every book I could access and learning about who I am as an African American man born within the hypocrisy of America. I watched *Roots* and *Shaka Zulu* for the first time, and those movies exposed me to the pride and dehumanization that my people experienced. I knew about slavery. I was aware of how Black people were forced into slavery, but I never knew my identity beyond who society decided I was going to be. I also learned about the 13th Amendment of the United States of America which, contrary to what's taught in school, did not "abolish" slavery or involuntary servitude. It merely rerouted that evil into what's now known as the criminal justice system. It was a bitter pill to swallow upon realizing that I allowed myself to become a "legal" slave! Before incarceration, I didn't know about African dynasties and Nubian Kings and Queens. Hell, prior to prison, I wasn't even aware that Egypt was actually a part of Africa. I was brainwashed to believe that Charlton Heston was the image of Moses and Yul Brynner was the likeness of Pharaoh Ramses.

 I learned about the resources within the African soil and how the earliest traces of humanity were found on the African continent. I had awakened from the slumber that generated dreams of self-hatred and stolen identity. For the first time in my life, I was proud of who I was. I was proud of my black skin and my lineage. I began to see other African inmates as my brothers. That didn't mean we'd all sit on the yard singing "Kumbaya" together, but I vowed to give them the benefit of the doubt.

 As self-awareness and self-pride were taking root within me, a disdain was as well. I no longer had the desire to inflict violence on another Black man. My angst and anger were directed toward everyone the represented the corrupt system in which I was entangled. The dark truth had emerged: I began to feel that everyone, from the warden's

CHAPTER 6

office, the parole board, as well as the Corrections officers, were all a part of an evil system designed to keep Black and Brown people oppressed. Outside of prison, it was more covert, but inside the system, it was as clear as day. I would hear some of the Corrections officers call adult incarcerated men "boy" or saying things like, "you're in Ionia now! I-own-ya!" Or that they were "Massa." For the first time, I realized that slavery had never ended in America, it had just continued by way of the 13th Amendment via the Prison Industrial Complex.

I evolved into somewhat of a Black Nationalist within the prison system. I was a loaded weapon with the knowledge of the Black struggle at the hands of evil small-minded people, and I was ready to fire off. I was anxious to find ways to link up with like-minded dudes so as to receive and confer knowledge. I intentionally fellowshipped with the many different social and religious groups of Black men—the Moors, the Melanics, the many gang sects, etc.—and I encouraged them to dissipate the conflict that they thought they had with each other and channel that energy toward building a cohesive unit amongst all of the organizations. I reasoned that there is strength in numbers so together we could demand better treatment and living conditions.

If there were two inmates who had a problem with one other, it was understood that the problem was between those two and not the entire group. There were no more gang fights and groups of Black men trying to kill each other over affiliations—we would circle up the two men with the issue, give each of them a shank, and let them resolve the conflict on their own. We took back some of the power the system wanted to withhold from us. We experienced a little bit of peace within the one facility; the prayer was that our mindset germinated throughout the system. We created our own unwritten rules of engagement that we all came to abide by and respect.

The prison staff became threatened by our leadership, so we immediately became targets for the staff's retaliation. They didn't bother inmates who were fighting and hurting other inmates, they specifically wanted to eliminate the leaders and those who tried to achieve unity. The Corrections officers would write me up for frivolous reasons, most of which were downright false accusations. They would accuse me of planning a riot or coup, or defying commands—eventually, I racked so many tickets and violations that I was a prime candidate for the hole and a transfer to a "higher custody" facility–which simply meant more restrictive placement.

The straw that broke the camel's back was an incident I had with a racist correctional staff. The corrections officer approached the table where I sat in the cafeteria and demanded my ID while I was eating. I ignored him and continued to eat my food because I knew he was trying to provoke me.

Just two days prior to that incident, the same officer worked in my cellblock. I disagreed with an instruction he had given, and as a result, he yelled in my face, "You're

CHAPTER 6

in Ionia, you know what that means? I-own-ya!" I walked away from his stupidity but knew he'd be a problem for me at some point.

Meanwhile in the cafeteria, the officer yelled, "I'm giving you a direct order! Give me your ID." At this point, the dining hall, which held well over 100 or so inmates, had gotten quiet. I took out my ID and tossed it on the table. The ID hit the table and slid onto the floor. It was unintentional but that didn't matter to the officer. The inmates sitting at my table didn't make it any better as they started laughing, which of course made me laugh. At that point, the officer was visibly upset. He picked my ID up off of the floor, then ordered me to get up and walk over to the control center with him for a shakedown. As I got up and grabbed the food tray, he nudged me with his right shoulder in the back of my left shoulder in an attempt to provoke a confrontation right then and there.

"Move faster!" he said in a lowered voice.

I put my tray away and continued to walk out of the cafeteria toward the control center door. As soon as we got inside the doorway, he spun me around by the sleeve of my right arm and grabbed the front of my shirt near my throat.

He put the finger of his free hand in my face and said, "Nigga, the next time I order you to do something, you better do it."

I felt both anger and fear at that moment. Without any hesitation, I pushed his finger out of my face. The officer yelled, "Yeah boy! That's an assault, motherfucker!"

I knew there was no turning back, so I threw a quick combination of punches toward his head and face. The officer fell backward out of the control center door and fell to the ground. The shift lieutenant was standing right behind the desk to my left and witnessed the entire encounter yet didn't say anything until I decided to retaliate. The lieutenant pulled his panic button, which was really a string that hung off of all the staff's two-way radios. When someone pulled it, it alerted other officers to the emergency. I put my hands in the air as a gesture of surrender. I knew what was next. I was then cuffed and escorted to administrative segregation also known as "the hole."

* * *

Once I was in the hole, the transporting officers beat me for what seemed like forever. I was in handcuffs during the entire assault. Aside from bruised ribs and a nearly fractured wrist, they left me lying on the cell floor for a couple of days until the facilities nurse finally demanded that they take me to the prison infirmary for evaluation and treatment. I remained in the hole for about a year because of that incident. It was during this time that I began to have an introspective understanding of my situation. I witnessed other inmates lose their minds while in the hole. They were willing to do anything to get some type of attention or interaction, even if it was a negative encounter with staff. Some would bang their steel footlockers continuously, trigger the in-cell fire sprinkler system, or even attempt suicide all to get some

CHAPTER 6

sort of interaction from another human being. As a result, the inmate would oftentimes end up getting "gassed" (a sort of tear gas used by staff to make a prisoner comply), or they'd get themselves "rushed" by the "goon squad," which consisted of four or more huge male staff who donned riot shields, helmets, and steel-toed boots. An inmate would almost always end up in the infirmary after those types of encounters. In some twisted way though, the inmate most often felt that he got the attention he sought after all.

To keep my sanity, I decided to go on an introspective silence. I didn't speak to anyone, prisoner or staff. Instead, I read books and worked out. I thought of my son. *He must be so big by now. He probably is a little hell-raiser, too. I know that he's smart and talented. I'm going to make sure that I tell him that. He needs to know that he's valuable. He needs to know who he is.*

I wanted to do something different because I didn't want to lose my mind like so many others had. I listened to things going on around me, but I didn't allow it to penetrate my mind.

CHAPTER 7

I was eventually released from the hole. Due to the disciplinary actions against me by staff, I had once again racked up 35+ points. I guess the prison officials had gotten fed up, so they informed me that I'd be transferred to a level 5 custody facility. This was a common retaliatory practice by the MDOC prison administrators. When certain inmates became too influential in a facility, they often get transferred to a further and possibly more dangerous facility. I was moved to the infamous State Prison of Southern Michigan (Four-Block Jackson). Four-Block was a level five facility and one of the most dangerous prisons in Michigan. This was commonly referred to as the "Big House." I had heard stories about this place, and they were serious enough to send shivers up my spine. No matter how scared I was, I knew that survival was the only option.

Once I arrived at Four-Block, I was assigned to 53-3rd, which is the 53rd cell and 3rd gallery. I walked up all those

CHAPTER 7

stairs to get to my cell with my property, then I looked down to the floor and felt dizzy. It was just that high up! I've witnessed death and violence within the Jackson prison, and corruption and violence were prevalent throughout the MDOC. Every single day I had to be aware of my surroundings because drama and violence could and, most often, would jump off when it was least expected.

Then there were the homosexual predators who stalked and raped other inmates who they determined were weak or vulnerable. I mainly stayed to myself and minded my own business, which consisted of attending school or group programming, working out, or reading the thickest book I could find in the library. That was the way I survived, that was my escape. But, in prison just because one decides to avoid nonsense doesn't mean you'll be fine. Trouble still found me from time to time and when it did, I did my best to address the issue swiftly. One of my favorite sayings was, "I'm not a predator, but I'm definitely not prey either."

One of the programs within the prison system was called Assaultive Offender Therapy Program (AOP). It was designed for prisoners who had committed violent crimes, but it was a very strict program with little room for nonsense. I attended the sessions, only I didn't take them seriously. I challenged the therapists and didn't buy into the rhetoric that they would share our criminal stories and feelings each time during 'group.'

"If you could go back," the therapist asked, "What is something that you would have done differently the night you committed your offense?"

I reflected on the night at the playground in '87 when those dudes caught me slipping. I was walking through the playground unarmed and alone and karma caught up to me. I knew that I should've taken that ass-whooping for jack'n their dope like a man instead of deciding to retaliate. Instead of answering truthfully and introspectively, I decided to save face in front of the other inmates by playing the asshole role. "I would have smoked everybody who saw me!" I answered. I wanted to piss off all these white people who never walked a day in my shoes yet wanted to come in and psychoanalyze me. A look of disgust froze on the therapist's face.

I was not of the belief that the prison system was effective at rehabilitating inmates or "correcting" our unlawful behaviors, so why pretend otherwise? I thought Assaultive Offender Therapy was a joke, and I treated it as such. Due to my aggressive and often challenging disposition, I was kicked out of the program. At the time, I didn't care; I was sentenced to 18-30 years. The only thing I needed to learn was how to survive within the facility, not figure out how to be a better citizen outside those walls.

I continued to be myself, encouraging other Black men to be the best and strongest version of themselves despite the present situation we found ourselves in. And as expected, it rubbed the staff the wrong way. Within the many different facilities, I was housed, what I've found was, for the most

CHAPTER 7

part, the staff no matter the race or gender, had the same ugly attitude and mentality especially towards the Black prisoners. I was a strong-willed young black man, and that was a threat to them. I continued to rack up tickets from the staff, some I deserved, but many of them I didn't. The pattern was always the same: I would have conflicts with staff, get written up multiple times, end up in the hole a couple of times, and then get transferred to another prison. I was never at any one facility for more than two years. I took that long drive back and forth across the Mackinac so many times that I developed shoulder pain from being constantly shackled for so long.

I hated the system and everyone involved with it. It's a curse but also a blessing that I remained in prison for as long as I did. I was filled to the brim with disdain, anger and bitterness toward the system. And just as obvious as an old movie rerun, after a few years, I was transferred from four-block to a level 5 facility "up north" which is prison lingo describing all prisons situated across the Mackinac bridge. This cuts off familial visitation due to the distance they are from Wayne County, which is where most of the African American inmates, who make up the majority population, lives.

* * *

The prison experience is both stressful and violent, but there are some enlightening moments as well. There's always one situation that stands out from all of the craziness during every inmate's bid. I'm no different. The eye-opening "ah-ha" moment that I was blessed to survive caused me to honestly reflect on my life and ultimately change my thinking. Unfortunately, it wasn't long after my transfer from four-block that the intense harassment by the Corrections officers began. It's unwritten knowledge that the officers from the sending facility will oftentimes contact their counterparts at the receiving facility to keep harassing particular prisoners. Once again, I found myself in level 5 custody. I was in the hole within the Marquette Branch Prison (MBP). The corrections officers at the Marquette facility consisted of approximately 91% Caucasian males, yet the prison's population was about 70% African American men. I recall being one of several African American inmates escorted to the hole based on some racist staff claims that I and other inmates were attempting to incite a riot simply because we were contesting the prison's conditions. I was found guilty of the major misconduct charge, then placed in the hole for an undetermined amount of time.

The hole unit consisted of three tiers. I was assigned to a cell on the top third tier. The base tier cells were designated for suicidal and psychotic inmates. As a safety precaution, each base cell had a separate plexiglass door standing approximately two feet in front of the cell itself in case one of the mentally ill inmates tried to throw feces or urine at anyone passing by.

I battled with my own sanity while being placed in the hole, and I desperately clung to the slight glimmers of light

CHAPTER 7

that appeared in my life. I always thought of my son. One thing that brought my tortured soul joy was thinking about when I would mail my son math problems or ask him to write me a report on an event or person of historical significance. My mother would return it once completed (whenever she had mental clarity). I'd check his homework, grade it then mail it back to him.

I would often listen to my headphones pacing back and forth imagining what it would be like when I got home. Obviously, I wanted to hold my son, but I also couldn't wait to be reunited with the people I knew. I imagined walking through the door of my mother's house and everybody surrounding me, giving me money, and celebrating my return. I imagined a joyous and festive time with me as the guest of honor. Whatever it took, I knew that I couldn't succumb to the mental collapse I saw all around me. *"Whatever you do,* I thought, *"Don't lose your mind in here.*

***

There were quite a few inmates who had let go of sanity while doing their bid within "the belly of the beast." One such inmate was a Caucasian, who was extremely psychotic. He had once cut off his own testicles while doing time in the hole. Using the large steel footlocker within his cell, he slammed the heavy lid down on his scrotum. On another occasion, a general population inmate day porter, the inmate whose job assignment was to sweep, mop and clean the unit, slid a razor under his cell door. The Caucasian inmate used that same razor to slit open his lower abdomen and then he pulled out a portion of his intestines. Needless to say, he was immediately transported by chopper to the U of M University's hospital.

I can vividly recall the frightening and life-threatening event during my stint in the hole. It changed my way of thinking and, ultimately, my life's trajectory. Someone slid that very same inmate a book of matches, and what he did next was insane and almost cost several lives, including my own! One Friday evening, he did what most of us thought was a random act of destruction, but little did we know he had a devious plan working. He triggered the emergency in-cell fire sprinkler using the matches. He realized that it would take a few working days before the sprinkler system could refill its water supply after being triggered. Unfortunately for us, it was the weekend. As a result, there would be no available stored water to fight a unit fire until the following week.

That following Sunday morning, while pacing inside of my cell, I noticed a trickle of smoke coming up from the lower tiers. I yelled to another inmate housed on my tier, "Hey, Pork Chop! You see that smoke?"

He responded, "Yeah dawg, I wonder wassup wit that."

About 20 minutes later, I heard an officer screaming, "Fire! Fire! His cell is on fire!" The next sounds I heard were the unit sirens glaring and the clinging of the officers' keys. They frantically ran to each tier with brooms to reach over the railings attempting to open the large windows for

CHAPTER 7

circulation. At some point, one of the officers decided to open the glass containment door of the inmate's cell, and that trickle of smoke quickly turned into a plume. Now, with the windows open and the breeze circulating, things got bad quickly. The inmate had used his sink to soak both of his wool blankets and sheets. He placed his mattress on the floor under the steel bed frame and then draped the soaked bedding on top of it. Then he used the matches to ignite the flammable paint on the walls of his cell and slid under the bed, totally protected from the raging flames. At this point, the thick black chemically powered smoke had billowed up to the unit's ceiling. As I mentioned earlier, my cell was on the third tier which is the closest to the ceiling. It didn't take long before most of the inmates on my tier began kicking their cell bars, slamming the footlocker lids, and screaming in panic. I held my composure until the poisonous smoke began to envelop my entire cell. My panic kicked in when I had to lie on the cell floor trying to gasp for breathable air. With my face pressed against the cell floor, tears in my eyes, and the fear of my impending demise looming, I had a conversation with myself that went something like:

"Is this it? Am I about to die without even a fighting chance? This can't be it! I wanna live! I wanna live!"

As I stated, it was the weekend, so the staff had to get permission by phone from the warden to get us out of the unit and into the yard for air. At some point, the warden gave the "go-ahead," allowing the evacuation. I was somewhere between consciousness and semi-consciousness but remember hearing the cell door open and someone putting cuffs on my wrists, then dragging me outside. Eventually, I along with several other inmates was transported to the medical infirmary for smoke inhalation treatment. When I regained full consciousness, I revisited the one thing that replayed repeatedly in my mind—the "self-talk" that I had had during that harrowing experience. I now realized that fighting the system didn't mean jeopardizing my life or possible freedom in the process. Neither did it mean allowing myself to continually be placed into the system's inhumane hole units. I realized it was possible to stand for what was right, and at the same time, not allow myself to be placed in compromising predicaments any longer. I decided to establish new self-goals, and ultimately, new behaviors. I was no longer going to go toe-to-toe with the corrupt MDOC on every issue. My new mission? To make it out of "the belly of the beast" alive and in one piece.

CHAPTER 8

After the fire incident, it seemed as though all I could think of– morning, noon and night–was the new goal of eventually gaining parole. By this time, I had served about 17 years and had witnessed other inmates with cases similar to mine go up for a parole board hearing and have parole granted. My file was so thick with points, write-ups, etc. that I wondered how I would be able to prove that I could actually be a productive part of society. I couldn't change my past behavior or what was written about me–good or bad–so I realized that I had to become more strategic and intentional about my conduct.

I bit my tongue so much that I could probably tell you exactly what it tastes like. Staff would try to trigger me into a reaction, but I practiced self-control and discipline. That was a challenging aspect of growth, but it was necessary. I found myself meditating and even praying a lot more frequently, and I resolved to be in 100% control of my thoughts, words, and actions as best I could.

Despite my new self and subsequent change of behavior, the staff still had it out for me. They would randomly search my room, which was annoying, but they had the right to do so at any time. It was obvious that they were targeting me because the staff would search my bunk area as much as five times a week—for the other inmates, this would only happen about once or twice a week. I would get tickets for having an extra towel, for my bed not being made a certain way—anything they could conjure up to pick with me. Then they would write me up if my T.V. wasn't in the right place, or if the cord of my radio hung a certain way. Their retaliatory tactics bothered me, not only because they were being assholes, but because the tickets they would write resulted in the loss of privileges. I was enrolled in college courses at the time, but because of my tickets, I was no longer able to attend. Ninety-nine percent of the time, I would receive a "guilty" finding in their "kangaroo" court process which would be officiated by a Corrections officer who was a buddy of the staff who initially wrote the bogus infraction. I was furious, but I reminded myself that my goal was to get out of there. I made a decision that shocked the staff and even some of the inmates housed within my cubicle. My decision was a very bold move. My goal was to play a game of mental chess against my enemies which would result in one outcome—Me being left alone!

CHAPTER 8

Without any prior notice or forewarning, I stuffed my tape player, T.V., and radio into a pillowcase and marched to the case manager's office. I dumped everything out onto the floor and told him flatly, "All of this, you can destroy."

"What?" he asked. He swiftly grabbed my thick file, perused it, and responded, "Mr. Spratt, you've been locked up a very long time, are you sure you want to do that?"

"Yes," I confirmed.

He was so confused. He wrote me a receipt for everything I had given him, and I went back to my cubicle. The other inmates who shared my cubicle thought I was crazy, but I knew what I was doing. I was willing to give up the things that the staff had been able to use against me. They couldn't ticket me for things that I no longer had access to. I was willing to forego the temporary pleasure of entertainment so that I could ultimately be in control of my destiny and so that they could leave me alone.

Two days later, one of the staff members came into my bunk cubicle with a duffle bag. "Spratt, pack your things. You're getting ready to ride out." Another transfer. I guess the administration decided they didn't want me influencing other inmates at their facility. I had defied the system yet again by simply outwitting my opponents, so I had to go.

* * *

Despite being transferred to yet another prison, I had the God-given ability to connect with other inmates. They trusted and ultimately confided in me. A lot of them could tell that I wasn't sneaky or two-faced, and they opened the door to a lot of meaningful relationships and mentorship opportunities. Some would vent to me about a staff member, and I would show them how to file grievances instead of retaliating in violence. I'd even write a complaint if a dude couldn't read or write.

"But naw, Spratt! This mutherfucker keeps on fuckin with me and talking shit man!" one of my peers lamented to me.

"That is fucked up bro, but what good would it do if you caught another case over words from a clown? If your goal is to get out of here, you've got to move differently," I counseled. "Believe me, eventually, he's going to rub somebody else the wrong way, too. Let one of those Lifers handle that. All dogs will have their day brother-man."

It then dawned on me: I had become one of the old heads who had taken the time to invest in my character when I was a hot-headed youngster all those years ago. I wish I could have told those guys that the seeds they planted had taken root and sprouted. There were many inmates who would come to me for advice or just encouragement, and I tried my best to give them a positive answer that would ultimately shape them into better men.

My position as a role model made me question everything I had previously thought about myself. *Was I always a good person? Maybe I was always good, but I was never around anybody who nurtured the goodness within me.* Most of my life was lived around people who had their own agendas and expectations for how I was to live my life. Instead of focusing on all the negative things that I did prior to prison, I searched for the good that was always there. I never hurt children. I didn't believe in hurting women. I had a moral code that some guys in my neighborhood never considered, and I realized for the first time, that I wasn't all bad. Maybe I was always meant to be a leader and healer but never had the opportunity to do so.

I was developing into a strong Black man. I didn't compromise my morals for anyone. I didn't bow my head or grovel before staff; I knew who I was extended beyond the prison bars that held me physically captive. Even though I knew that the staff and administration had the upper hand, I knew they couldn't break me. My mind was free. It was strong. Nobody could take away the years of development and progress I had made. Once I was able to walk into my authentic self, doors began to open for me that were previously never an option.

By God's divine favor, I found myself back in Assaultive Offender Therapy. It was unheard of for an inmate to participate in the program a second time, but there I was. I was different, so my experience in the program was also different. I took it seriously. I was real, and I was starting to come to grips with who I was and what I wanted out of life. I found the sessions to be a lot more meaningful, and in some ways, a lot of the weight that I carried was lifted. I shared how my mother used to beat me—something I never told anyone else about—and I shared how I felt lonely and abandoned because my father wasn't in my life. Some guys in the group would go back and tell other inmates some of the intimate things I would share, but I didn't care. I had been a slave to my past for too long, and I was ready to part ways with it.

As always, I was viewed as a threat by staff. I threatened their job security. Not only did I decide that I was never going back to prison, but I also encouraged other inmates to adopt the same mentality. This goal became bigger than just me; I wanted to elevate my Black brothers and heal my community. It was my goal to leave as many empty beds and prison cells as possible. To threaten the livelihood of everyone connected with the Michigan Department of Corrections—everyone who made a profit off the backs of Black men. I wouldn't refer to myself as a male Harriet Tubman or anything like that, but I felt a great mandate to mentally emancipate as many as I could.

* * *

While I was undergoing a metamorphosis in prison, I learned that my brother was following in the footsteps I left behind. I learned that he was selling drugs and running with the wrong crowd, just as I had before. One day, I called my brother to see how he was doing and to possibly drop a seed that would change his mindset.

"Dell, I'm out here getting this money!" he laughed. "When you come home, I'mma put you back on. It's me and you!"

I was so detached from that lifestyle that hearing him speak about the "game" in that way was a chilling reminder of my younger self and an abandoned mentality.

"Naw man," I chuckled. "I'm going to come back and sit my ass down somewhere!"

My brother laughed again, and we ended our conversation shortly after. I needed to reach him. I wanted to rescue him because I didn't want him to be robbed of so many years and time away from what mattered most. I had to bookmark my mission to save him until I could at least save myself.

* * *

A dude from my hood came into the "weight pit" where I was working out and told me that my uncle had just rode in. My uncle and I had been housed at the same facility before in the past, but this time felt a little different. I had some new and exciting news to share with him. I was eager to explain my newfound way of thinking and moving.

On that fateful day in June 1987, we both made a conscious decision to act both reckless and impulsive—not having a care or consideration for human life in those fleeting moments. I truly regret my actions, and if it were possible, I'd change things in a heartbeat. I regretted reuniting with my uncle under those sorts of circumstances, but there's one thing life had taught me, you gotta take the bitter with the sweet.

"Unk, I know I said this before," I began, "but dawg, if only I wasn't such a hothead back then!"

"It ain't yo fault nephew," he assured me. "I got away with all kinds of shit in them streets! Our case ain't the reason I'm here. They wanted me off the streets a long time ago. Karma is a bitch!"

Although I was a juvenile in June 1987, I still felt sort of responsible for our situation. Yet, on the other hand, because I revered him so much, had my uncle given me an instruction not to react the way that I did, I would not have pulled the trigger that day.

* * *

"Mr. Spratt," the case manager called out to me in passing. I was on the way to chow when he told me something that would change the trajectory of my life forever. "You have a parole hearing coming up this week."

I felt the warmth of optimism overtake me. This was a chance to prove that I was capable of being an asset to society and that I was fit to be released. I didn't know if they would be willing to listen to me since all the other times, I was denied parole, but I had progressed into someone different. Maybe they would be able to see that.

My optimism lasted well up until it was time to meet the board again. I was bound by shackles with a look of dejection on my face. I always thought how intentional it was for the Corrections officers to present you this way to the parole board. First appearances are lasting. I was

CHAPTER 8

presented to them looking as though I was coming from the "hole" for an assault or something worse, when prior to the meeting, I was walking around the yard and housing unit unrestrained. When I walked into the meeting room, I saw my file, thick as a thief, sitting on the table. I didn't know how I would be able to defend everything that was there, but I was willing.

I sat awaiting the board's arrival when two Black women entered the room.

"How are you doing Mr. Spratt?" one of the women began.

"I'm fine, thank you. How are you?"

"Good."

They sifted through my file and began reading some of the write-ups I had received.

"Can I say something, Mr. Spratt?" the more seasoned of the two began. I later found out that she was the sister of a well-known Detroit City Council member and she, herself, had been a prominent politician as well. "You're not still sitting here in those prison blues because of your initial charge. I get it, you were young and from inner city Detroit, I really believe you made a terrible mistake and served the time for that offense."

I perked up because I had never heard a parole board member say that to me before. Before I could get too excited, she continued. "You're here because of this file. This file is almost three inches thick."

I felt my stomach drop. I listened to what she said and agreed that there was a lot there. I was ready to defend myself still, and I asked God to give me the words to say in that moment.

"Ma'am, I understand what you're saying," I began. "As you can see, I am an A-prefix, which means that I had never been to prison before. I was 17 and a half when I came here, and I have been to some of the worst prisons in Michigan. Up until now, I've never been to any of the so-called 'easy' prisons, or anything remotely close to it. I've been across the Mackinaw bridge more times than I can count."

I took a deep breath and stuffed down my emotions and continued to plead my case. "That file does not reflect who I am; it reflects who you are supposed to be when you come to prison—what your expectations are when you come here. That file is only me managing expectations."

Their eyes were razor-focused on me. Before, I could tell that the board members really didn't care to hear what I had to say, but this time was different. And since I knew I had a captive audience, I continued. "I am not a predator, but I'm damn sure not prey. I had to do what I had to do to survive."

The senior member of the two Black women sat up and replied, "Hmm. I see that you were in Assaultive Offender Therapy in Munising level 5, and you were kicked out Is that correct?"

"Yes, I was," I confessed, but I don't think I was given a fair shot that time. I don't want to go into detail because

CHAPTER 8

I don't want it to sound like an excuse, but I wasn't treated fairly."

"Ok," she continued. "I see that you're now enrolled for a second time. You know, Mr. Spratt, you're very lucky. You're only supposed to go through AOP one time within the MDOC."

"I know," I agreed. "I don't know what happened, but I'm using this opportunity wisely."

She looked curiously at me, studied my file again, and then spoke. "I'll tell you what, Mr. Spratt. I'm going to hold off on your parole decision until you complete therapy. I want you to mail me the results once you're finished."

"You want me to mail it directly to you," I clarified.

"Yep," she confirmed. She gave me the direct address and told me that she would render her decision as soon as she receives the copy of my A.O.P completion.

Is this real? I thought to myself as we concluded the session. I was now more determined than ever to leave for good. It wasn't long before I finished therapy, and I immediately mailed her the results, as agreed upon. I was ready to go home. It was now a waiting game. I had already served nearly 19 years, what's a few more months?

CHAPTER 9

While still awaiting the board's decision, I was transferred to Coldwater, a level 1 facility. This was my first and only experience at a level one facility and it was starkly different from what I had come accustomed to. It was relaxed and mirrored society more realistically. We would see regular people (civilians) walking about like they were just walking outside of the mall. From time to time, women would get our attention by flashing their breasts at us while driving past the 14ft. high yard fencing in their convertibles. It was weird but not unwelcome. To pass the anxious time I'd do what I had become accustomed to doing: either working out or reading. One day, as I was working out, the counselor called me to his office. "You ready to go home, Mr. Spratt?" He asked cheerfully.

As soon as he asked me that question, I began to weep. I don't know where they came from, but the tears formed as if they had a mind of their own. I couldn't control them

CHAPTER 9

and I don't think I would even if I could. Every pain, every lesson, every loss, even the small gains, all led me to this one fateful moment. My emotions were confusing because I had nothing on the outside of those walls. What home would I even return to? Besides my son, who was waiting for me? But I knew that I would rather sleep on a park bench than spend another day in the hellhole that was my home for over 19 years. I had survived a place where men suffered at the perverted and twisted whim of other men so I was all too ready to face the next chapter of my life.

The counselor went on to explain how my parole came with a caveat: I had to complete a re-entry program in Jackson Prison. The reason being, I served so much time as a first time felon, that the MDOC wanted to "ensure my successful transition." *Bullshit!* I thought. But if it meant exiting the "belly of the beast," I was ready to go.

"I want to warn you Mr. Spratt," the counselor continued, "They tend to put the most hard-nosed corrections officers within those units. If you break any rule, they will give you a duffle bag and a wagon, send you packing to a regular housing unit, and cancel your parole. Go over there, lay low, and get out of there."

I was grateful for his advice. I appreciated the "heads up." I now knew what to expect when I got there and like that old Schoolhouse Rock commercial I used to watch as a kid on Saturday mornings used to emphasize, "knowing is half the battle." Shortly after that conversation, I was transferred to the Jackson Cotton Facility (JCF) "Reentry

Program Unit." When I arrived, I was given a wristband that indicated my release date. It had to be visible at all times, and if it wasn't, that would be considered an infraction. Mine read "2.14.2006." That was going to be the best Valentine's Day of my life; there was no way in hell I would get this close and blow it. The problem with the wristbands is that all the other inmates could see your parole date, too. A guy could be sitting down eating his food, when another inmate, who had a life or a surplus of years, would see the release date and come swinging just to sabotage any chance of his release so, the name of the game was to stay vigilant and low key. Being in the reentry unit was like walking on eggshells every day; anything or anybody could jeopardize my chance at parole.

There were so many rules and procedures we had to adhere to, that it almost seemed like they were designed for inmates to fail! There was no smoking, which was okay because I didn't smoke anyway, but other rules just didn't make any sense. For example: after we made our beds in the morning, we couldn't sit on them until after 8 p.m. at night. I was there long enough to see plenty of inmates take the "walk of shame" back to the regular units, losing their proposed parole date simply because they failed at some minor aspect of the re-entry program rules.

To help assist me with successfully completing the program, I put in a request to see the deputy warden. This particular administrator had literally witnessed me grow up

CHAPTER 9

from a young man into a full grown adult within the MDOC as she worked at several of the prisons where I was housed during my incarceration.

"Wow, Mr. Spratt, you've gotten older," she began the conversation.

"Yeah, I know. You've known me a long time, Dep, and out of all the years I've been in the system, you know I've never requested to meet with you before now."

"Yes, I was amazed to receive a call out request from you!"

"I wanted to speak to you not just on my own behalf, but for every man that is housed within the Re-entry Program Unit. I need for you to explain to me the purpose of having the meanest, foulest officers in a unit where every man is preparing for release in the next four months or less? We all have release dates displayed on our wristbands. Prison is already traumatic enough without our feeling as though we were walking on eggshells daily within a unit that was supposedly created to prepare us for release. Why have men re-enter the community filled with pent-up anger, fear, and stress? I think that's a recipe for failure and disaster for both society and the parolee—wouldn't you agree?"

She sat back in her chair and pondered my point of view before responding. "Mr. Spratt, I appreciate what you're saying. I don't have the ability to make any changes to that program but, I'll take your feedback to the personnel in charge of the community corrections program for consideration."

I left her office hoping that I had made some sort of impact, but I figured that nothing I said would really matter in the end.

Despite the fact I didn't want any sort of work assignment while housed in that unit, I was given one anyway. I was assigned to be a day porter —someone who cleans the bathrooms and shower areas—and I hated it. I would have to work all day for twelve cents an hour. I had no choice but to accept the assignment. Refusal would be considered disobeying a direct order, which would sabotage my parole. I had to change my mindset regarding the assignment. I would scrub the toilets and clean the showers with pride—not because I liked cleaning up after other grown ass men, but not only did I deserve to use a clean toilet, but the few guys I had a rapport with did as well. I would become exhausted cleaning the bathrooms, only to have a corrections officer come to my cell and ask me why they weren't clean. When I would go back to investigate my work, there would be tissue and paper towels everywhere. It would look worse than it did before I cleaned it. *This is my test*, I thought to myself. I endured this minor irritation and did my job to the best of my ability every day. Although I didn't have a stable home to parole to, I was determined to complete the goal of getting the hell out of the "belly of the beast!" even if it meant paroling into a halfway house.

My time in the re-entry program crawled by, but at some point, I stopped both looking at the calendar and counting the days. I didn't want to torture myself obsessing over every day, hour, minute, and second until I was able to leave. One morning, as I was laying on my bunk reading, a Corrections officer approached my bunk area and said, "Spratt, in the morning, pack up and take all of your blankets and shit to the Quartermaster then report to the control center. You're paroling out tomorrow."

I jumped up and looked at the calendar. Had that much time really passed? I had finally found myself arriving at February 14, 2006—I was excited, but I was an anxious mess. All day, I watched my back and kept to myself so nobody would notice that I was scheduled to leave the next day. I got along with most of the men in the unit, but I couldn't afford for anybody to involve me in any bullshit this day. If I had come this far and wasn't able to leave, I don't know what would have happened to me psychologically. I stayed up all night waiting for someone to call my name so that I could finally expand my wings and take flight into the great unknown.

The next morning, I took my sheets, pillowcases, laundry, and extra "state blues," down to the Quartermaster for turn in. Once I arrived at the prison's control center, I noticed several other men standing around, all with that look of anxious relief. The Corrections officers escorted us through the corridor under the basement over to the dress-out room. There were khakis and a button-up shirt available for me to change into. Taking off the blue jumpsuit felt like a metamorphosis: like a peeling away of the old self and stepping into promise and possibilities. I wish I could have burned that jumpsuit. I made a decision several years prior that if this day had ever come, I'd never allow myself to be put in a position where I'd have to wear that symbol of slavery, shame and despair ever again.

Even with new "parole-out" clothing, I didn't think this was actually happening. I was expecting to get right to the door only to find it locked and a Corrections officer signaling me to come back into the control center for one reason or another. The Corrections officers continued to escort us outside to the sally port, but without handcuffs. I felt a mild panic attack erupt within my brain, chest and body. Once outside though, it might sound silly, but somehow the air smelled different, cleaner. We walked through the prison's security gate and marched onto a Greyhound bus.

"Gentlemen, you can sit anywhere you would like," the driver instructed us. I looked around, and there were no shackled, uniformed prisoners. There were only *civilians*. Regular, free people. I sat next to a lady, making sure to give her as much space as she needed so as not to feel uncomfortable then, just like that, the return ride back to Detroit nearly 20 years later began. I still have that Greyhound bus ticket to document the day that I departed an old life and was rebirthed into a new one.

* * *

After arriving at the Greyhound station in Detroit, it seemed like time had just shot by, but I was standing still. The city looked so different, and the people looked strange to me.

CHAPTER 9

There were clothes and cars that I hadn't seen before, and people using what I came to learn were cell phones, iPods, and other devices. As I continued to look around, I saw a gorgeous woman walking toward me talking and smiling. I was thinking, *Oh damn, I don't know her but she on me like dots on domino's for real!* Before I could even ask her name, she walked right past me as if I wasn't even standing there. I was confused. As I became more acclimated to my newfound freedom, I learned that she was having a conversation via Bluetooth. I had to laugh at myself.

I continued to people-watch and take in the view of the city until my younger brother arrived to pick me up and drive me to the "halfway house" on East Jefferson & Lillibridge St., I thought to myself, this must be how my foremothers and fathers felt after being fre*ed from bondage.* The feelings of uncertainty, unfamiliarity, and fear. I thought of those last Texas slaves who were freed on Juneteenth who wondered: "I'm free! But what do we do now?" I didn't know anything else but being told what to do and when to do it. There was an immediate culture shock. It didn't take reality long before it slapped me right in the face. Eventually, I would have to feed, clothe, and house myself. For 20 years, the Michigan Department of Corrections had done that job, and now, on my first day as an independent man, I didn't know how I would do that. Sure, I knew how to sell dope and make money 20 years ago, but that was no longer an option or my desire. Besides, I had been out of the game for so long that I didn't even know how things operated now.

For the first time in years, I was afraid. Like I did as a young boy, I channeled that fear into aggression for survival. People hear stories all the time about the horrors of prison, but in prison, we also heard stories about how crazy the world had become. I had stepped into unfamiliar territory, and I wasn't sure how I could thrive in it. My faith was low. I believed in a Higher Power, but I didn't have enough of a relationship to realize that it was actually that Higher Power that not only sustained me through it all but has also guided me thus far. I arrogantly believed that it was my wit, my strategies, and my cunning alone that got me through.

I also hadn't considered the family of the person I killed and how they had dealt with his death all these years. I wondered if they would still recognize me, and if they did, would they seek their own retribution? I was 100% remorseful for what I had done, but I knew that my remorse wouldn't bring their loved one back.

Though I was afraid and stressed and every other emotion in between, I was also open to new possibilities and excited to learn, grow, and navigate this new world. Despite feeling out of my element, I knew that the uncertainty of my place in life was better than the familiarity of life as an inmate.

CHAPTER 10

My time at the halfway house was relatively smooth but by no means perfect. I got along with the staff, and the other residents respected me. Some of them knew me from either the joint or my past life in the streets, and because I was in prison for nearly 19 and a half calendar years, most of the younger guys recognized me as an "OG" or a "Big Unk." There were strict rules and expectations, even more than I experienced in prison, so I was a little confused. How did I leave an environment that monitored and controlled me just to end up in another place that was *more* restrictive? There were curfews, drug tests, rules for this or that—I knew that I didn't want to be here long and that there had to be a way for me to live a more normal "civilian life." But where would I go?

The worst thing about living in the halfway house was the filth. Even when I was in prison, I made sure that my cell was clean. I would take Irish Spring soap and use it to mop my floor just so I could have that "fresh out-doors" smell. A mantra one "ole head" taught me a while ago that really stuck with me was, "Cleanliness is next to Godliness." I kept my shoes lined up neatly, and as much as I could control in terms of cleanliness and tidiness, I did. I believe I developed a case of undiagnosed OCD.

The other men in the halfway house really didn't care about the upkeep; I guess because they knew that they would be there temporarily, it didn't matter how they lived. The person who was assigned to clean the bathrooms would do a half-assed job, so there was soap scum and a strong, pissy odor that dominated the space. I would never walk into the showers barefoot, but even when I wore shower shoes, I wanted to throw them away afterward. The state of the communal bathroom was obviously terrible, but there would be guys who stood in there eating donuts and drinking their coffee while having a full conversation with another man who'd be sitting on the toilet doing his business. I don't know if being institutionalized made those guys comfortable, but I thank YAHWEH that he didn't allow me to think that type of behavior was normal.

Outside of the halfway house I was aware of glimpses of institutionalization in my behavior as well. I noticed how difficult It was for me to make some decisions on my own. I didn't realize until then just how many major and minor parts of my life were decided by others. I remember chillin over my brother's house, when I asked him what time we were going to eat.

CHAPTER 10

"If you hungry, go in the fridge and get you something to eat!" he laughed. "You don't have to wait for me, bro!" That was an eye-opener for me. The small luxury of eating what I wanted whenever I wanted was a privilege that I didn't appreciate before prison.

Hearing the loud jingling of a key cluster was a trigger that I had to work very hard to control as a result of being institutionalized. That was one of the torture tools of the sadistic Corrections officers. They'd purposely walk past your cell during a security count round rattling that damn key cluster as loud as they could at 2 a.m. or 3 a.m. to deprive the intended target of any sleep. They would also flash their lights into our cells directly into our faces while they did their rounds. It was a Pavlovian response: I was classically conditioned to feel anxious and annoyed by the keys, and I hated that I was still feeling the effects of my oppressors' sadistic tactics.

Despite the conditions of the halfway house and my difficulties integrating into "normal" society, I felt that something positive was going on. I felt that my life was climbing upward. Even though my surroundings didn't indicate that, the change within myself was enough to keep me pushing forward.

* * *

Not long after I was paroled out of prison, I decided that it was time to reunite with my son. I reached out to his mom so that I could see him. He and his mom drove from Rochester,

NY to visit me at my brother's home. Neither of us could contain our excitement.

"Dad..." he could barely get out before he ran into my embrace, faster than any Olympic track star. We were finally able to be in the presence of one another without bars, security glass, and overseers. I hugged him tightly for what seemed to be forever. It took me back to that Wayne County Jail visiting cell where a jail sheriff with a huge heart afforded me the opportunity to hold my infant son during a family visit. At that time, I was facing a possible "natural life" sentence.

"You're a man, now," I uttered to him–a shocking revelation, but also a sad one. He was grown now, and I had been a distant bystander throughout his growth process. What challenges had he faced since I wasn't present to guide him into manhood? If I was present, what type of man would he be. It's a catch 22: had I been in his life without a renewed mind and living my old lifestyle, I probably would have damaged him. At the same time, being absent all his life was also damaging. I was determined to pick up the pieces and to be present for him as much as my son needed me to be. I was going to be a father to him no matter what it took. Our relationship continued to blossom and it wasn't long before we fell into the typical father/son relationship where I gave sound advice and he ignored most of it. Happy isn't a big enough word to describe my feelings.

There was still another person who I needed to see again: my mother. Because I was subjected to an extreme number

CHAPTER 10

of transfers during my prison bit, coupled with the fact my mother was frequently moving from rental to rental due to her addictions, our communication was nearly nonexistent. Still, she was my mother, and I wanted to honor her, so I asked my brother if he knew where she was. He didn't, but after enough asking around my old hood, I was directed to a shabby apartment building on Detroit's southwest side of town near the Ambassador bridge. I told my son, who was visiting from New York, to accompany me so that he could have some time with his grandmother.

The visit was nothing like we expected. I knocked on the door and I heard the faint attempt of my mother trying to answer.

"Ma, it's Dell! You alright!" I yelled.

Then there was another unclear response.

I knocked again, "Ma, open the door!" I tried to open the door to come in, but the chain prevented me from entering.

Immediately, I decided to break the door down. When my son and I found her, she was naked and swollen lying on her couch. She couldn't muster the strength to sit up and get off the couch. The strong smell of urine alerted me to the fact that she had used the bathroom on herself; in all my years, I had never seen my mother like this weak and defeated. We searched for a gown to put on her while I attempted to figure out what was going on with her.

"Ma, what's your doctor's number?" I asked in a panic.

"Motherfucker, you not about to call my goddamn doctor!"

I ignored her and searched for her medication which had the doctor's phone number printed on the label. My son was putting on her socks and shoes so that we could take her to the hospital while I talked to the doctor.

"Mr. Spratt, I told your mother back in December that her kidneys were only functioning at five percent. She needs to start dialysis and I haven't seen her." The doctor told me further details about her condition, and soon we transported her to his office. My mom stayed in the back with her primary care provider for what seemed like four and a half hours before he came out and said frankly, "Mr. Spratt, if you love your mom, you need to take her to Botsford hospital immediately. She needs to start the dialysis process to save her life!"

* * *

I spent time going back and forth checking on my mom, but other than that, I didn't have much time to fraternize outside of the halfway house. Even still, my brother would often pick me up sometimes to catch up and see how I was doing. I had changed drastically since the last time he had seen me, but it was difficult for him to accept all the ways that I had evolved.

"Dell, we are about to get this money!" he declared excitedly as I sat on the passenger side of his car. "It's me and you against the world!"

"Bro, I told you I left all that behind me years ago. That street shit ain't for me no more, dawg."

CHAPTER 10

A look of confusion and disappointment spread across my brother's face, and then it turned to anger. "Nigga what you mean, it ain't for you? You and Unk ran shit like a king in these streets when y'all was out here! I got the connects. Ya little bro making moves out here now. I'mma put you all the way on, just say the word!"

"You hanging on to a ghost, little bro!" I yelled back at him. "The big bro you remember that was out here ripping and running the streets is *dead*! I'm not him no more, so I don't give a damn about your connections, dawg."

He was crushed. In his anger and pain, he called me everything except a child of YAHWEH—almost as if I wasn't his brother. Like I didn't mean shit to him at that moment. It was hard to digest his words, and I wanted to beat his ass every time he would go there with me. Something inside would remind me that my brother wasn't mentally or spiritually capable of appreciating who I had become yet. I understood that. I had to stay consistent in my change so I would not only garner his respect but also so that maybe my courage to change would rub off on my little brother whom I loved dearly.

* * *

I knew of several men who got out trying to lay their "gorilla hand" back down in the streets only to end up wheelchair-bound, permanently paralyzed, or worse. One day I got off the bus and started walking on Michigan Ave. headed to the social security office to get a new card. A nice BMW pulled up alongside me, and when the tinted window went down, I recognized the gold toothed smile of one of the dudes I grew up around from my hood.

"Whatupdoe?!" He asked.

"What's good, dawg?!" I replied.

After a few minutes of catching up, he let me know that he respected me for being a solid "stand up" dude before and during my prison stretch. Sounding concerned, he asked how was I getting along. I had to admit that it wasn't a cakewalk. I needed things and hadn't secured a job as of yet. I was even having a tough time trying to get all of the documents together needed to prove my identity so as to get an I.D.

"Creating a life from scratch is tough bro!" I told him.

Homeboy said, "Hold on, dawg," then started rummaging through his center console. After a minute, he said, "Here ya go dawg" and handed me a rubber banded roll of money with a slip of white paper attached. "Get at me, homeboy."

I responded, "Good looking out, bro! I'mma pop at'cha playa." He drove off and I felt conflicted. I mean, I had enough money now to buy a few essentials but his number on that white sliver of paper really bothered me. I really hate to be put into a situation where I'm made to feel obligated to someone just because I'm in need. It just didn't sit well with me at all.

That number burned in my pocket for weeks. It seemed like the solution was written in black and white. Despite

CHAPTER 10

the temptation, I told myself I'd give the "right way" a real try before I went there. The thought of possibly going back within the system was sickening.

Eventually, one of my mother's older brothers found out I had paroled and that I might've needed a place to stay. He extended a room in his home to me until I got on my feet. The offer was weird because I remembered that this particular uncle and I never really liked one another when I was a kid.

Although I never really trusted my uncle growing up, I knew I needed a place to stay. *I can work through this* I thought.

Though I appreciated that he gave me a place to live for a while, it was a very tumultuous time under the same roof with him. He was very restrictive and told me I could only take two showers a week because daily showering would put too much of a strain on the water bill. He owned a two-family flat, so after he left the house, I would go upstairs to the second apartment and wash up in the sink. Somehow, he found out that not only was I showering two days out of the week downstairs, but I was also "washing up" in the sink upstairs the remaining five. He was furious. I came back to the house from a parole office visit and went upstairs to wash up only to find that my uncle had duck taped the sink and attached a sign that read "DO NOT USE SINK, PIPES MUST BE REPLACED!!!" I just stood there in disbelief. *His house, his rules,* I thought.

I knew I needed to get myself together and get on my feet so I could get my own shit! There was a beautiful church around the corner from my uncle's home on the corner of Conner & Jefferson Ave. named Historic East Lake Baptist Church; I had to pass every time I got off of the bus returning to my uncle's home. The huge church billboard always displayed inspirational quotes. One Thursday night, I was so bored and in need of a spiritual refuel that I decided to put on my clothes and visit that church. Maybe it was time to re-establish my relationship with God. I wasn't a Christian, but this was a place where Black people were talking about God. I felt like I belonged, so I went to investigate.

I walked into Historic East Lake Baptist church during Bible Study and was amazed at how crowded it was. I didn't know anyone and didn't want to be noticed, so I sat in the back. I didn't know what to expect. I felt small, but a brother sitting next to me welcomed me by offering to share his Bible. I read the scriptures and listened to the pastor's words of wisdom and was impressed—it seemed like he was talking directly to me, and I was all ears.

"It doesn't matter what your circumstances are or what you've done in the past, God still has a plan for your life! You can't just have faith, you need to have actions, too!"

This message resonated with my soul. I felt a tug on my heart, so I raised my hand to speak. The pastor acknowledged me, and I began to tell my story.

"How y'all doing? My name is LarDell. I just got out of prison a few months ago after serving nearly 20 years,

CHAPTER 10

and to be honest, I'm lost. I'm torn in different directions. I don't want to go back to prison, but life is proving to be very difficult. Honestly, I'm running outta options at this point."

There was lots of encouragement from the congregation, and Pastor Cunningham told me to meet with him in his office directly after Bible Study. After the service was over, several people approached me—well-meaning—but I wasn't seeking any attention from them. They were congratulating me and giving kind words, but I didn't buy into any of it. It was hard to gauge whether or not they were sincere, although I do believe most of them were. Honestly though, I didn't care. My focus was the Pastor and his wisdom.

As I continued to make my way to the front of the church, I heard a woman say, "Brother LarDell, God's got a plan for you." I looked in the direction of the voice and saw a red-headed, light-complected woman with gorgeous copper freckles. She had a pair of the most beautiful big eyes I'd ever seen. It was in those eyes that I saw her spirit, her humanity, and her sincerity. Smiling, the sister resumed putting her Bible and belongings into her large purse. Afterward, the sister began walking toward me. I felt a little boyishly nervous but enjoyed watching her every stride toward me.

"I'm Sister Nita," she said. Nita's perfume complimented that moment so perfectly. I later found out it is her signature scent: Clinique Aromatics Elixir.

"I'm Dell. Nice to meet you Sister Nita," I replied.

"God has great things in store for you brother Dell. He brought you out for a reason" she said, then she spontaneously hugged me.

I was uncomfortable at first. This was the first time I had touched a woman in nearly 20 years. Although I was uneasy, Nita's presence was calming, and she told me again, "God's got a plan for your life." There was something deep and unexplainable in her eyes that kindled something inside of me. I felt Sister Nita's spirit, it was very strong. She definitely stood out from all the other women in the room. I know this sounds crazy but, somehow, I sensed that we would be connected in some way.

When I entered Pastor Cunningham's office, I was amazed at how cultured he was. I was so used to seeing images of white Jesus and naked white angels floating around every church; I appreciated the African art that he had prominently displayed on the walls. That night I shared so many experiences with him, and he listened to me for as long as I needed him to. He offered advice and support, and it felt good to have someone I could share the burden of the last 19 years with. What stood out the most during our conversations was how Pastor Cunningham, a highly intellectual and well-to-do gentleman, never talked down to me or made me feel less than. Instead, we simply spoke as two Black Men who respected each other's points of view and convictions.

Pastor Cunningham and I are still good friends—even today. I wasn't used to being close to other men—I didn't

CHAPTER 10

trust many. All of the men who were a part of my life when I was growing up were negative influences and steered me down a dark path. Pastor Cunningham was genuine and he encouraged me to be the best version of myself that I possibly could. For a while, I couldn't receive all the good things he would say about me, but he was consistent and he helped me build my confidence. He is one of the heroes in my story who extended his arm to someone who was sinking in quicksand and needed help. I am forever grateful.

CHAPTER 11

Although I found myself thinking of Nita often, I didn't have any plans of getting into a serious relationship. My son's mother had several other children during my incarceration which hurt me deeply. As a result, I tend to put up a wall of protection around my heart toward females in general. Once I paroled my plan for women was simple: "Hit'em and quit'em" using protection, of course because they couldn't be trusted. But the more I talked to Pastor Cunningham and came around the church, the more I wanted to get to know Nita.

Eventually, I found myself attending church every Thursday and Sunday. I was intent on getting Nita to like me, so I got baptized, joined the choir, and did anything else I could do to impress her. I wasn't really sold on church or Christianity, it was just an act for Nita. If they needed me to put on a chicken suit and spin a sign on the corner, I would have if it meant I'd be in Nita's presence. My plan to be a

CHAPTER 11

heartless womanizer went completely out of the door! All I wanted to do was be a part of Nita's life. Although I was only focused on carrying out my personal plan of winning Sister Nita over, God was secretly working on my heart. I was going through the motions for Nita's sake, but in the process, I was also opening my heart to true friendships and fellowship. Unfortunately, up until that point, life had consistently taught me that no one could be trusted. But the church gave me a sense of community and family that I had always desired. I finally felt safe enough to lay down the sword and shield I created to protect my physical and inner self. I was in no way naïve, I was aware of the fact the church is like a hospital in that, only the sick and the suffering are admitted. With that said, I also realized that although I was enjoying my newfound sense of community, that community consisted of recovering addicts, street walkers, liars, fornicators, thieves and sociopaths so I never expected perfection.

***

I had finally mustered up the courage to pursue Nita. One Bible study night, I put my plan into motion. I still lived right around the corner with my uncle, so I asked Nita if she would drop me off at home. She agreed, and we hopped in her little black Ford Focus, heading for my uncle's house.

Once we pulled up in front of the house, I began to tell Nita how I felt: "Sister Nita, I'm really feeling you. I hope that's ok to say."

She glanced in my direction and then smiled. "That's ok," she responded. "You're nice, but I'm in the process of ending a serious long term relationship so, I'm not looking for anything like that right now."

Damn. That's not the answer I was hoping for, but I respected her honesty. What more could I ask for? I discovered that Sister Nita was a few years older than me and had more experience with long-term relationships. She was definitely more mature than I was, so when she said that she wasn't ready, I didn't press her.

She didn't cut me too deep though. Before I got out of the car she said, "But I'll still be your church sister! If you need anything and I can help, just let me know". I was content with that.

Sister Nita invited me to several church-related events, and although I would feel a little awkward, she would make her way to wherever I was sitting and check on me. She was there when I needed her—just like she promised. She would sometimes take me to my mandatory parole office visits, grocery shopping, and doctors' appointments. I didn't want her to think I was taking advantage of her, so I made sure that I offered gas money, but she wouldn't accept my help. It was hard being around Sister Nita while merely in the "friend zone". I had the most amazing times with her, and she never made me feel like she was better than me or that I was anything other than a Black Man.

I respected that Sister Nita didn't want to get involved romantically, but a few months had passed since we began hanging around each other. and I couldn't ignore my feelings so I thought that I'd give it another try. Hey! I'm a man, don't judge me.

"Hey Nita, if you don't have anything to do tonight, do you want to watch a movie?"

"Yes, that sounds nice. What time shall I come over?" she asked.

I wasn't expecting this to happen, but I was so glad she said "yes." She came to my uncle's house, and I put on a movie that I really didn't care to watch. I was more interested in some intimate conversation with Sister Nita. I paid attention to everything about her. *Does she feel comfortable? Is she feeling me, too? Am I being too aggressive?* Once we were about halfway into the movie, I moved closer to Nita. I quickly gauged her response to make sure that I wasn't moving too fast. She didn't seem bothered, so I moved closer again.

"Nita, is it ok if I kiss you?"

She looked at me curiously, smiled, and said, "That's fine."

We were inseparable after that. Our relationship continued to grow. Even though Nita gave me no reason to doubt her feelings for me, I felt inadequate. Here she was, a hard-working woman from middle-class upbringing who pretty much had her life together. *Who am I?* I thought. A jobless and homeless ex-con on parole who didn't have much going for myself or much to offer anyone. Still, Nita didn't make me feel inadequate. She was always encouraging, making me feel like I was worthy and valuable.

* * *

As Nita and I grew closer and dated for a few more months, she decided that it was time for me to meet some of her close friends and family. First, she and her friend, Loretta, came to my uncle's house so that Loretta could check me out; I had a bouquet of flowers waiting for them. When I saw that Loretta was with her, I picked two of the prettiest flowers from the bouquet and headed outside to greet them both. As soon as I got to the car, Nita introduced me to Loretta and vice versa. Afterward, I handed each one of the ladies a beautiful red rose. I could tell that Loretta had already warmed up to me and that made me feel accomplished. We sat and talked for about an hour. Shortly after Nita and Loretta left, Nita called and told me that Loretta thought I was a nice guy and that she approved of me. *Yes! I was in!*

We took a different approach to meet Nita's family, and for good reason. Nita gave me some advice that was challenging to hear, but I understood her reasoning.

"Dell, when you meet my family, don't tell them that you spent 20 years in prison yet."

"What you mean?" I shot back at her. "That's a part of who I am! If they can't accept me for me, then I don't want anything to do with them!"

"Calm down," she advised. "I understand what you mean. I just want them to get to know who you are first

CHAPTER 11

before they learn about that part of your life. If you show them the good, decent man that I already know you are, then they will be able to better understand and accept your past."

She was right.

We decided to keep my past a secret until her parents got to know the real me. I came to affectionately know my mother-in-law as "Mama Connie" and her husband as "Papa Joe" (R.I.P.). Once Nita and I were confident her parents had accepted that I'd be hanging around awhile, we decided it was time to have the conversation about my past with them. Surprisingly, it went very well.

Mama Connie said, "Dell, I would've never guessed you been to prison, especially for 20 years."

Papa Joe simply said, "You got a fresh start, everybody deserves a second chance."

That was it. Next was my stepdaughter and a host of aunts and uncles. To this day, Nita's family has never made me feel like anything but family.

***

Nita was a bright light in my life, but I quickly realized that I didn't want to snuff out her light with my darkness. Though I had made considerable progress mentally and emotionally, I realized that I still had a lot of anger that was steeped in fear. At one point, Nita didn't even like to go out in public with me because I was so aggressive toward people I perceived as threats. One time we were at the movies, and I didn't like the way that a guy was looking at me.

"The fuck you looking at?" I snapped at him.

"You good. I ain't got no beef!" he raised his hands and chuckled as a sign that he meant no harm. I looked at Nita, and she was pissed and embarrassed.

"I'm not going anywhere else with you if that's how you're going to be," she warned.

She had every right to feel that way. I did some inquiring about mental health programs and started therapy. I didn't want to lose Nita, but I didn't want to lose myself and allow my fears, temper and impulsivity to lead my back down a path that I vowed to never travel again.

* * *

Dating Nita opened up a whole new world of experiences and opportunities. Before meeting her, I had never been beyond the west side of Detroit. She took me to a carnival on 12 Mile and Hoover—in Warren, MI—and I was amazed to have even traveled that far. Nita is also responsible for my first experience with seafood at Red Lobster. We ordered shrimp, but instead of only eating the meaty parts, I was munching on the shells like they were chips.

"Oh, no! What are you doing?" Nita giggled.

"What?" I asked, guarded.

"You know you're not supposed to eat the tails, right?"

"Oh." If I were light skinned, I know I would have turned red. We both laughed, and even though she teased me about the shrimp a few times after that, it was in humor.

CHAPTER 11

The more I spent time with Nita and immersed myself into her world, the more I was sure I wanted to be with her for the rest of my life. I hadn't dated any other women since I'd been home from prison, but there was no need to try to explore any other options. I realized we had only been dating a couple months and I can only imagine what people would say, but *fuck them* I said to myself–Nita was "it" for me. There were only three things I needed to know before I decided that I would ask Nita to marry me. When I found an opportunity to ask her, I did.

"Hey Nita, I have a few questions for you," I told her while we were sitting in the car.

"Okay." She responded.

"Do you believe in God?" I asked.

I could tell that the question threw her off-guard. She answered anyway, but curiously. "Yes, but you know that, Dell."

"Okay," I did a mental note. "The next question: do you smoke or do drugs?"

"No!" she laughed and playfully tapped my arm. "Why did you ask me that?" Nita asked.

"I'm just making sure I ask the right questions." I felt like a prosecutor interrogating a witness. I had to make sure that I was making the right decision, even though I was 99% sure.

"Okay, last one," I continued. "Do you like to hang out at night and go to clubs?"

"No," she answered confidently. "I guess I'm kind of boring."

"Boring is good!" I reassured her, and I meant it. Though I didn't have much experience with dating in my adult years, I knew enough to know that I wanted a God-fearing, wholesome woman. I didn't want a woman who lived a risky, extravagant lifestyle or one whose integrity would be in question later. I had done enough thrill-seeking in my youth to last a lifetime. I wanted emotional safety, stability, and in the best definition possible, predictability.

"Nita, you're everything I want in a woman, and I hope I'm what you want in a man. I'd like to marry you."

She didn't cry, scream and shout "yes!" like they do in the movies. She looked at me stately and responded, "But you barely even know me."

"I know enough," I reassured her. "The three questions I asked you were important to me, and you confirmed what I already know about you. Anything else, we can learn about each other as we grow."

Nita agreed to marry me. We were married by Pastor Michael G. Cunningham on February 18, 2007, right after church services at Historic Eastlake Baptist Church. It was a simple yet beautiful ceremony. My brother was the Best Man and my stepdaughter, the Maid of Honor. Several of our friends and family were in attendance, but nothing could compare to the sight of my beautiful bride upon the opening of the sanctuary doors. Nita was glowing. I was emotional. All of a sudden, a song that only Nita knew was special to

CHAPTER 11

me began blasting through the PA system just as the double doors of the church's sanctuary flung open to present a gorgeous Nita and her stepfather preparing to begin her journey toward me. "I am ready for love," India Arie began to croon, and I couldn't hold back the waterworks. Nita gracefully began to walk toward me, and it was at that point that I began to feel worthy.

We needed to make a lot of adjustments to balance our relationship; I quickly realized that marriage was both a mirror and a magnifying glass. Before Nita, I had only been with girls. Girls were fairly easy to impress—if I bought them nice things, they were submissive to me. They never questioned me, and we never had any real goals besides sex, partying, fresh gear, and more sex. Nita was not like them. I had to earn her respect and trust. She spoke her mind when things didn't seem right to her, or if I was flat-out wrong.

We loved each other and had great times in our marriage, but because I had spent nearly 20 years without interacting with women, I was lacking in my understanding of relationships. For example: when Nita and I first got married, we had sex all the time. I think many newlyweds can attest to how fun the honeymoon stage of marriage can be, but I didn't understand that there was more to marriage than sex, hugs, and giggles. I was always ready to be physically intimate, but there were times when Nita wasn't. I knew my wife's intimate desire for me hadn't changed, but I couldn't figure out what the problem was. I selfishly felt things could not go on like that for much longer.

In my frustration with our sex life, I went to Pastor Cunningham to express my frustration and to ask him what I should do to get Nita to be more sexual with me.

"We used to do it all the time," I lamented. "Now it's like she's not matching my energy level."

"What you have to understand, Lardell, is that you and Nita have not matured at the same pace spiritually, mentally or sexually." Pastor Cunningham began. "You spent nearly 20 calendar years having to suppress your sexual appetite. Sister Nita experienced sex and relationships in a healthier and more mature way. So, as you get older, your sexual appetite tapers off. I don't think that she's intentionally withholding intimacy. It's going to take some compromise and understanding on your part, Lardell. You're going to have to mentally mature and find positive ways to release that energy. Find a good gym. Always remember, sex is merely a small part of the necessary ingredients for a good marriage."

I was expecting him to take my side and agree that Nita was wrong, but he didn't. People who genuinely care about you won't always agree with you, and that's why I appreciate Pastor Cunningham. Even though I was making progress in my mental, spiritual, and emotional well-being, I realized that the 17-year-old boy inside of me still needed healing as well. My journey to wholeness didn't end with Nita, I still had quite a journey ahead of me.

CHAPTER 12

As a man and husband, I didn't feel comfortable with my wife being the only one going to work every day and providing for us, so in addition to the odd jobs I was working, I decided to apply to a temp agency, for a job. I'd been denied so many times by employers because of that damned question on the application: "Have you ever been convicted of a felony? If yes, explain." I figured I had nothing to lose by applying somewhere else one more time. The temp service accepted me as an employment client and sent me to my first full-time paid assignment. It was a plant on East Eleven Mile Rd. and Groesbeck Hwy. I met with the plant's manager who told me that all I would have to do is work at a location for six months with good attendance and I would be hired as a full-time employee. I would work like a Hebrew slave every day for a laughable wage, and before six months were up, the temp service reassigned me to a new location. This meant I got the exact same "six-month permanent hire" speech from the new plant manager. This treatment would go on several more times. I was pissed. Later, I learned that the company didn't want to hire me because I was an ex-offender. Though I was upset at their discriminatory policies, I would not let that stop me from making something of myself.

I was still on parole and meeting with my parole officer regularly; it was through one of those meetings that I connected with Mr. Vance G. who gave me my first real full-time job as a second shift unit manager at an all-male parole facility on Gratiot Ave. The facility was owned by the Traveler's Aid Society of Metropolitan Detroit. Travelers Aid had a contract with the MDOC to house parolees for at least ninety days and to offer services to help them become independent. I didn't understand how I was supposed to be in charge of parolees while being a parolee myself. The job paid $10 per hour, significantly more than the $7.25 per hour at the temp agency. Working with Mr. Vance G. within that facility helped me to reframe my thinking and shift from being an ex-offender to a civilian. Once I learned that I would have to drug test each parolee's urine when they returned from a home visit, some of my old prison thoughts tried to dominate.

"Man, I ain't doing that old police-ass shit!" I protested.

"You can't think of it like that Spratt," Mr. Vance G. explained. "Listen, you ain't in prison no mo.' You ain't a criminal no mo' right? This is your job bro".

"Right," I confirmed.

CHAPTER 12

"This is merely a part of your job," Vance continued. "Part of your job is to keep this facility safe. Addiction is serious, and some of these guys need our help. Their addictions go against the progress they're trying to make."

It all clicked for me after that. I ran the facility with a different mindset—I wanted to run it with integrity and in a way that would cause the other men to respect me. I was able to walk that very thin line where the men respected me as a legit staff yet, they didn't look at me as a rat or a bootlicker. I developed some genuine relationships because I cared about everyone I was assigned to. I excelled at my position, and I came to see myself as more than just someone working a job; I was a professional.

Working with Mr. Vance G. and the team at the center was a rewarding experience. The parolees housed there definitely helped me to become a better professional. In turn, I like to think I helped them realize that despite being labeled "parolees," "ex-cons," or "criminals," with a little faith and investment in self, one could still etch out a good life. I still had this feeling that I wasn't doing enough though. I mean, I was doing what a man is supposed to do, but I knew that I needed to do more. I needed to give back to the community that I took so much from as a misguided youth.

I spoke with Vance about my desire, and he had a suggestion: "Well Spratt, you don't make much money, so financial donations are out. How about volunteering a little of your time?"

"How?" I eagerly inquired. Vance went on to suggest things like serving food at a soup kitchen or offering help at a local shelter. I was sold!

I ran the idea of me volunteering by Nita, and she encouraged me to find a cause that I cared about. After some searching, I decided to contact the Neighborhood Service Organization's Tumaini Center (Swahili for "Hope") which was on 3rd and Martin Luther King Jr. Blvd. The Tumaini Center was a homeless shelter. After a week or so, I received an invitation to come into the shelter for an interview. Almost immediately, they cleared me to work as a volunteer at the homeless shelter. I felt accomplished.

The first day I walked into the facility, there was an overwhelming stench of decay. It was a hot and humid midday which definitely did not help matters. I felt myself becoming sick because the smell was so unbearable, but I knew that these people were vulnerable and needed help. It was my calling. Instead of beds, there was a sea of chairs; a lot of the homeless clients slept outside in the Cass Corridor area which came to be known as "Tent City." Tent City wasn't technically our jurisdiction, but what happened there also affected our clients. I noticed that some people had visible ailments and infections. Most people would see a situation like this and turn the other way, but I knew that there were far fewer people willing to stick it out and assist this vulnerable population of displaced people. I had to be one of them. It was so amazing to talk to residents and hear their stories—hell, I

CHAPTER 12

was just in their shoes not too long ago. After volunteering for a few months, I was offered a paid position as a Client Advocate. I received a gleaming recommendation from Mr. Vance G., Pastor Cunningham, and even my mean-ass parole officer, I was offered a $15 an-hour position as a Tumaini Center staff member.

My experience with NSO was one of the highlights of my professional experiences. It felt good to be able to contribute financially to our household and help my wife with the bills. Beyond that, I not only felt valued by the company, but I also felt that the work I did was making an impact on the people I served every day. One day during my shift, I received a surprise visit from the CEO herself, Mrs. S. Clay.

I didn't know what to expect when I arrived for the meeting with Mrs. Clay. Although a couple of years had passed since I was hired at NSO, and though I believed that during that short time I performed my duties above what was expected, I was still nervous. *Shit, are they trying to fire me?* I thought as I waited for Ms. Clay to call me into her office.

"Mr. Spratt, come on in!" Ms. Clay summoned me. "I know you didn't think I knew who you are, "but I've been getting very positive reports about what you've been doing for our organization."

Little ol' me with just a GED was meeting with the CEO of a major organization. I smiled humbly and said, "Thank you, so much ma'am. It's been a pleasure working here."

"Our clients have been talking about how considerate and compassionate you are with them, and the staff has been singing your praises to me for a while now."

I was at ease knowing that this meeting had a positive tone and that I wouldn't be packing my things into a cardboard box to take home.

"There is a supervisor position that's going to be available soon," she continued, "and I want you to apply for it."

"Thank you so much, Ms. Clay, but I don't think I'm the right person for that position." I don't know why I was playing myself so small. I obviously still needed to build my confidence.

"Why not," she looked, puzzled.

"Well, there are others who have been here longer than I have, and I don't have much experience as a supervisor. They didn't even give me a good job in prison—"

"Mr. Spratt," she interrupted me. This time she enunciated so that I could understand her clearly, "*I want you to apply.* Your mistakes and humility are what make you valuable here."

I applied, as Ms. Clay requested, and, to my surprise, I got the second-shift supervisor position. I didn't realize how important the supervisor was in maintaining the safety of the facility. I confiscated a gun and several knives from clients who had grievances with other clients and planned to hurt them within the facility. There was one homeless family who sold drugs across the street from the facility in the vicious Tent City area. That family made it challenging

CHAPTER 12

to not only keep the other clients safe but to also keep their drugs out of the facility.

"Mr. Spratt, Mr. Spratt!" one of the clients rushed into my office. His face was visibly full of fear, so I shot up from behind my desk to see what the problem was. "They gonna kill him out there!"

There was a gay couple who lived in our unit, but they would also visit Tent City to get liquor and narcotics or whatever else was available to indulge in. The infamous drug-dealing family that lived there tricked the couple into coming over for drinks this particular day, but soon after, the family started beating them both with tire irons. The only reason for this assault was homophobia.

One of the men who was assaulted managed to get away and ran into our unit. He was bruised and dripping blood from everywhere. I grabbed one of the ladies who was on shift that day to assist him and to call 911. They sat him down and wrapped his head up while I went outside to diffuse the situation with the other victim.

"Mike!" I yelled out to the assailant. He was beating the other gay man mercilessly. "Let him go, Mike!"

"Man, Mr. Spratt, this ain't got nothing to do with you! This ain't y'all business! I'm outside! I'm not in the unit!" he scoffed and continued to brutalize his victim. "These gay muthafuckers gon' learn."

"Okay, Mike, you proved your point," I was desperate to find a way to get him to stop. "What are you going to do? Catch a murder case? There are 200 witnesses out here."

Mike hesitated for a moment but would not let his victim go. I continued to try to convince him to stop. "Look at your knuckles. You got blood all over them. You need to go to the hospital to make sure that you didn't get exposed to any viral infections while you out here assaulting folks."

His eyes got big, and that was all I needed to say to convince him to release his victim. I didn't know if the gay men had HIV, AIDS, or any other autoimmune disease, but I had used Mike's homophobia against him to save their lives.

There were countless other dangerous situations that occurred, but thanks to the ongoing training and drills that were sponsored by the NSO, I felt both confident and prepared for any situation that may have arisen. Working at NSO was so rewarding, but it was also challenging. I worked at the Tumaini Center for several years before transitioning into a case manager position for the EFFECT program funded by Wayne State University. The purpose of this program was to investigate and prevent recidivism, the tendency for male offenders to reoffend, in ex-offenders. The EFFECT program identified three factors that contributed to recidivism that occurred before, during, or after prison:

1. untreated mental illness
2. untreated substance abuse
3. untreated physical disability/illness.

This mission was something that I believed in wholeheartedly: to keep my brothers out of the criminal justice system. I had

CHAPTER 12

seen all the horrors of prison life and the effect that it had on communities. Even as an inmate, my goal was to create as many empty prison beds as possible. I was only one person, but I wanted to completely dismantle and restructure the criminal/justice system. It was and still is steeped in racism and capitalism. How can justice be for profit? If it is for profit, how can it be just?

Sometime later, I found out that due to my background as an ex-offender and the work that I had done prior to EFFECT, I was hand-picked for the case manager position for the EFFECT program. The position with EFFECT was a significant increase in pay in benefits and I only had one person to report to. I had my own office and had a lot of input in day-to-day operations of the program. I could tell that some of the program directors were nervous about servicing ex-offenders, but I wasn't. I was responsible for running a support group for our clients twice a week and then I would report their progress to their probation/parole officers. In the first group I attended, I ran into some guys that I had met while I was in prison.

"Spratt! What's good!" Melvin shouted as soon as he saw me.

"I'm good man, how you been?" I hugged him before we began the session.

"Shit, not as good as you! How you get to be a part of this bro? Plug me in, baby! Give me the hook-up!"

"I got here through hard work and consistency, my man," I shared. I couldn't give Melvin the "homie hook-up" because it's not a real thing. It does not exist! I told him, "Dawg, imma give you the real 411...you ready?" He nodded that he was. "Here it is bro...Arm yourself with as much knowledge as you can so you'll be marketable. Make yourself marketable."

Marvin started laughing and said, "Maaan, whatever!"

* * *

I spread my wings and worked for other organizations and programs, but I found myself coming back to NSO multiple times. The rule was that you could only return after leaving NSO twice before you became ineligible for any further employment. Despite the rules, Ms. Clay allowed me to return a few times. Several years later, after we both had moved on from NSO, Mrs. Clay explained to me, "Many people thought that I showed you favoritism, but it wasn't that at all. You were a good employee! You were great with the clients, and you earned everything that you were given. If you wanted to come back, I would be a fool not to let you." I felt flattered.

While at NSO I also worked part-time at a youth detention/treatment center in Highland Park as a youth advocate as well. The NSO did allow me to obtain credentials as a Social Service Technician License, and I also became a mental health peer support specialist during my tenure. Because I was working in housing, I was also sent to Lansing, MI to train as a licensed housing inspector.

CHAPTER 12

I would have never thought that a past as stained as mine would open so many doors for me. I think back to what Ms. Clay, the CEO of NSO once told me when she met me: "Your mistakes are what make you valuable." She was right, but I would venture to say that it wasn't just my mistakes, it is the willingness to learn from and not repeat them. I no longer had the number in my pocket to get back into the drug game. There was no longer a need for it. I would never return to the destructive life that previously befell me. I was living life and life more abundantly.

CHAPTER 13

Even though so many things were happening for me professionally, my mother's health was rapidly declining, and I needed to figure out the best course of action for her care. The doctors said that she was no longer able to live alone, and she refused to live with me and my wife, so I had to put her in a nursing home.

The hardest thing in the world for me was becoming her legal guardian. She had me on an emotional rollercoaster. My wife and I would visit to check on her, and at first, she would be as sweet as pie. Then she would change her tone completely.

"Mutherfucker, you ain't shit!"

Though she was disabled and weakened, she still had a psychological hold on me. She stirred up the same feelings of inadequacy and fear that I had experienced as a child, only I was a grown man. She was fragile, but she still had power over me.

CHAPTER 13

I decided that I needed my brother to help me with her. We were riding in his car together when I expressed my frustration with his lack of involvement with my mother.

"Dude, you don't never come up to the nursing home. They don't even know that she got another son. All you do is ask her for money, so she sends me to the bank to withdraw money just to give to you! I need help with momma."

"Man, I was doing it when you was locked up!" He barked back at me. "You don't know what I went through!"

"Yea, but I was the one getting beat!" Those old wounds came completely to the surface, and it was like we were kids again.

"Dell, you received the abuse, but I had to watch it. I had to watch my mother beat my brother damn near half to death and I couldn't do nothing. What do you think that did to me?"

I had no response. It was one thing for me to endure the physical aspect of our upbringing, but I hadn't thought about how much he also suffered. It was the first vulnerable moment we had, and I wished that I would have spent more time with him when we were kids. All I showed him was how to be a thug, just like my uncle had shown me. Rather than being jealous and aggressive toward him, I wish that we could have connected better. I loved him dearly, but I really didn't know him.

Boo was heavy in the street game, so I tried to give him some money from time-to-time to tie him over so that he didn't have to get out there and sell drugs. Sometimes he would accept the money, and other times he would cuss me out because he figured that we should be together making money in the streets. It became a pattern of making up and toxic conversations and it got to the point that I didn't want anything to do with him.

* * *

In May of 2010 I awakened from a dream that was so realistic. I was sobbing. I could not explain it any other way other than my soul was grieving. I was at a church looking at a stained-glass window and the sun shined through it. I was facing the audience; they were all looking at me as I attempted to sing a song in front of them. As I tried to sing "This Little Light of Mine," it was hard to catch my breath, but I knew I had to finish the song. The sadness of that dream was so overwhelming that even though I was awake, it took a while before I could calm down.

Nita rolled over and asked if I were okay. After I told her about the dream, she handed me a pamphlet that contained scriptures and spiritual encouragement and asked me to read it when I had downtime at work. I was still unsettled, but by the time I arrived at work, I managed to calm my mind. I was still working for the NSO, supervising the homeless shelter; it was a pretty easy-going day. By the time 10:00 pm rolled around, I received a devastating phone call.

"Dell! Boo just got shot!" his wife called me in a panic. She went on to explain the details of the incident to me.

CHAPTER 13

"Where is he now?" I asked her, already picking up my things and preparing to rush out to him.

"He's sitting up against the garage."

According to my brother's wife, someone started shooting at him from the abandoned house next door. One of the bullets went through his garage and struck him in his back and caused damage to his internal organs.

"Tell him I'm on the way! Is he in pain?"

"No, he said he's not in pain; he's just very hot." She responded.

I told my staff that I had an emergency and darted out of the building as fast as I could. On the way, I kept reassuring myself that he would be fine. *That's Boo, he'll be alright.* I dashed up the street, hitting potholes as big as craters, and when I arrived at their house, the front end of my car was torn up.

"They already took him to the hospital!" his sister-in-law informed me when I arrived. I jumped back in my car and dashed to Sinai Grace hospital. I seen my nephew standing somberly outside of the hospital. "He gone, Unk.".

"I ain't tryna hear that nephew," I protested. "Where's my brother?"

I ran into the hospital demanding to see my brother. Initially, the hospital staff tried to prevent me from seeing him.

"Y'all not gon' tell me I can't see my brother!" I roared at everybody in earshot. "we slept in the same bed and ate out of the same bowl. I don't care what condition he's in, let me see brother...NOW!" After a few moments, the hospital staff took me to the small room where my brother still lay on the gurney with the oxygen tube still taped to his mouth. A part of me died as well. I held his hand and kissed the top of his head as I always done. I headed back to the room where the rest of his family was waiting.

A priest came into the room so as to console everyone, but I sat to myself. Then all of a sudden, it hit me—the dream! It was the most eerie feeling, but I believe that God was preparing me for what was about to happen. I probably would have lost my mind had I not already been emotionally prepared. Even through tragedy, God has a heart and he cares about ours as well.

In the midst of my grief, I felt rage shoot through me being. My brother mentioned having problems with a local drug dealer continuing to sell drugs literally in front of his home, putting him and his family at serious risk. My brother didn't want any drama from someone thinking that the dealer actually lived there. He confronted the guy and for awhile the dealer found another place to sell his dope. Unfortunately, it wasn't long before the punk started selling in front of my brother's home again. Once again little bro confronted him but this time the encounter had a deadly ending. I wish I had more time to simply convince my brother to move his family away. I miss my little brother dearly. Words cannot express the loss I feel in my heart daily.

On the day of my brother's funeral service, I followed the dream exactly. Brother Austin, the choir director at

CHAPTER 13

my wife's church was on the keyboard, and I walked up to sing "This Little Light of Mine." Then it clicked: in the dream, It was difficult to breathe while I was singing—my brother had difficulty breathing because he was shot. As I sung, I noticed how the people looked up at me and how the sun shined through the stained-glass window—just like in the dream. I knew I had to do it. I knew for some reason, this dream had to be fulfilled.

I have so many childhood regrets. I never meant to let him down. As much as I wanted a different life for him, I had to respect his choices. He was comfortable with his decisions, so I had no choice but to be comfortable with his choices as well. Unfortunately, our knowledge of one another was limited as we didn't hangout much growing up, but our love was expansive.

* * *

Due to my mother's failing mental and physical health, I became her guardian, and placed her into a senior living facility in Warren, MI. My mother was finally settling down in the senior home, despite the fact she scared several of the nurses who worked there. At one point, everyone was on edge because she was aggressive and threatening. Eventually, she came to love the staff, and they loved her back. That was my wish for her. For her to be surrounded by love and peace at some point in her life. I forgave my mother for all the things she did to me, though I still deal with the remnants of them.

In 2011, I received a call that my mother had passed away from complications of renal failure. I was at peace with her passing. One of the last times we visited, she told me that she loved me and that she was proud of me. I had never heard her say anything close to that before. I didn't realize how impactful her love was until I could feel the little boy inside of me begin to heal. I made sure she had a beautiful funeral ceremony.

AFTERWORD: UP FROM ASHES

I've always identified with the story of the fiery Phoenix, the bird that sprung up from the ashes. The fiery bird that sprung forth from nothing—from deadness—and shows itself to be alive and well, and strong and thriving. That's how I see my life. When I decided to start my business, I knew that Up from Ashes would be an appropriate name. You need the ash and you need the fire to emerge. You have to have the nothingness, turmoil, and chaos; then you have to have the pathway out.

My experiences have paved the way for me to touch the lives of countless others. Up from Ashes encompasses motivational speaking, life coaching, and mentorship. The goal is to show others that it doesn't matter where you begin in life, some more disadvantaged than others, you can always arise.

I wish the man I am today could talk to the boy I was yesterday. If I had a positive male role model pouring into me, I know I would have made different decisions and could have bypassed a lot of the pain and trials that I've endured. But yet, I am here: stronger than I ever was. Despite all the mistakes I've made, God's hand was still on my life.

In some ways, I want to thank my former self. Had little Lardell not made the mistakes he made, the current Lardell wouldn't be here and wouldn't have had the opportunities that I've had. I also wouldn't have had a heart for advocacy and to uplift my community had I not been immersed in the horrors of my circumstances. I believe that there are no strange happenings. I wish that my trajectory in life wasn't at the expense of someone else's life, but I believe everything that happened served a greater purpose. I believe that we all reap what we sow: I took somebody's brother, and as a result, my brother was taken from me.

I miss my brother. To an extent, I still feel responsible for the life he chose, and part of me will always wish that things could have been different. Now I am in a position to save someone else's brother from going down a similar path and helping someone else choose life.

I forgive my mother. I needed to give her that gift more than she probably needed to receive it. Because I have released the pain and anger that she had a major part in developing within me, I am now free to love. I can trust my wife with my heart. I can support and nurture my children and grandchildren. Though I am far from the perfect husband and father, I can be a source of encouragement and strength. I can break the curses that threatened to attach themselves to my future begotten generations.

I have been blessed with spiritual glasses. Once I decided to put them on, I opened myself to the realness of the world. I can't give the glasses away to anyone to see what I've seen or to see things the way I see them; at best, I can explain my beliefs and guide people to an enlightening spiritual path. I am up from ashes.

ACKNOWLEDGMENTS

I give the highest praises to my Heavenly Baba without whom nothing is possible.

Words cannot express the Love and admiration that I have for my wife Sharnita. Bae, your patience, encouragement, and devotion to both me and our marriage is inspirational.

I could not have undertaken this journey without the assistance of Tucker Publishing House, LLC. Coach Tara, I really appreciate your knowledge, expertise and drive to help others heal through the written word. Just as invaluable was the literary input of "lil" Evelyn.

Also important to this project was Attorney Mikai Green of GreenLaw. Your legal expertise and advice was greatly appreciated, Sis.

Additionally, this endeavor would not have been completed without the mentorship of Sheilah Clay (Former CEO/President of N.S.O), and the Neighborhood Service

ACKNOWLEDGMENTS

Organization. Mrs. Clay, thanks for seeing in me what I couldn't see in myself.

To my guy Vance Gerald (Formerly of Beyond The Gates). "One-Love" my friend, till we meet again.

I want to acknowledge Noble Drew Ali and the M.S.T. of A, Inc. It was within that organization I received invaluable guidance into both spiritual and cultural awareness during the earlier years of incarceration.

My deepest appreciation goes out to Pastor Michael G Cunningham (Historic EastLake Baptist Church). Words cannot express the Love and admiration that I have for you big bro!

A sincere "thank you" goes out to Pastor Charles Winfield (Fresh Start Ministries). Your wise words and encouragement are appreciated my friend.

I would be remiss if I didn't acknowledge my mom, "Big Dollie" as well as my little brother affectionately known as "Boo". I really miss you both dearly. I take comfort in knowing that you both are in the presence of the Almighty where there's no more pain, grief, or disappointments. Until we meet again.

To my son, Laron, grandchildren, nephews (both biological and adopted), nieces, uncles, aunts, cousins, to all of my "in-law" family by marriage, friends, co-workers and supporters, thank you!

To all of the haters, doubters, and detractors past and present, thank you! You all are literally the fuel that drives my determination to succeed.

Lastly, I want to acknowledge—ME! I had to unearth a lot of painful memories and traumatic events that were buried deep for this project to reach completion. I was the obedient servant! I stayed the course! I am truly: Up From Ashes!

AUTHOR BIO

Lardell L. Spratt, affectionately called "Coach Dell," was born in the City of Detroit, a City he still calls home. He is a licensed Social Service Technician and holds a Certified Peer Support Specialist Certification. He also possesses a Master Life Coaching Certification from an accredited I.C.F training program. Coach Dell is a community activist and a proud member of the Detroit 300, a group committed to ensure the safety of women, seniors and children.

With several years of experience working within the Social Service field, Coach Dell has served the dual diagnosed (D.D) population as well as the long/short term homeless and severely mentally ill populations. He has also had the opportunity to work with at-risk youth within one of the largest youth treatment facilities in Highland Park, MI.

Coach Dell is a very spiritual man who has a strong connection to YAHWEH and the ancestors. He is a proud husband, father and father figure, brother, granddad, uncle, and friend.